THE GRAMMAR GUIDEBOOK:

A COMPLETE REFERENCE TOOL FOR YOUNG WRITERS, ASPIRING RHETORICIANS, AND ANYONE ELSE WHO NEEDS TO UNDERSTAND HOW ENGLISH WORKS

Also by Susan Wise Bauer

The Writing With Ease Series
(Well-Trained Mind Press, 2008-2010)

The Writing With Skill Series
(Well-Trained Mind Press, 2012-2013)

The Story of Western Science:
From the Writings of Aristotle to the Big Bang Theory
(W.W. Norton, 2015)

The Well-Educated Mind:
A Guide to the Classical Education You Never Had
updated & expanded ed. (W.W. Norton, 2015)

The Story of the World: History for the Classical Child
(Well-Trained Mind Press)
Volume I: Ancient Times, rev. ed. (2006)
Volume II: The Middle Ages, rev. ed. (2007)
Volume III: Early Modern Times (2003)
Volume IV: The Modern Age (2004)

The History of the World Series
(W.W. Norton)
The History of the Ancient World (2007)
The History of the Medieval World (2010)
The History of the Renaissance World (2013)

WITH JESSIE WISE
The Well-Trained Mind: A Guide to Classical Education at Home, 4th ed.
(W.W. Norton, 2016)

THE GRAMMAR GUIDEBOOK

ARTICLE · ADJ · ADJ · N · PREP · OBJ OF PREP · PRES PART (ADJ) · N (PL)

A Complete Reference Tool for Young Writers, Aspiring Rhetoricians,

CONJ · INDEF PRO · ADJ · RELATIVE PRO · V (ACT) · INFIN (AS N; DO) · ADV · N (PROPER) · V (ACT)

and Anyone Else Who Needs to Understand How English Works

BY SUSAN WISE BAUER

WELL-TRAINED MIND PRESS

Publisher's Cataloging-In-Publication Data

(Prepared by The Donohue Group, Inc.)

Names: Bauer, Susan Wise, author.

Title: The grammar guidebook : a complete reference tool for young writers,
aspiring rhetoricians, and anyone else who needs to understand how
English works / by Susan Wise Bauer.

Other Titles: Complete reference tool for young writers, aspiring
rhetoricians, and anyone else who needs to understand how English works

Description: [Charles City, Virginia] : Well-Trained Mind Press, [2019]
| Previously published as: Grammar for the well-trained mind.
Comprehensive handbook of rules. ©2017. | For instructors and students of
grades 5 and above. | Includes index.

Identifiers: ISBN 9781945841576 | ISBN 9781945841583 (ebook)

Subjects: LCSH: English language--Grammar, Comparative--Study and
teaching (Middle school) | English language--Grammar, Comparative--
Study and teaching (Secondary) | English language--Rhetoric--Study and
teaching (Middle school) | English language--Rhetoric--Study and teaching
(Secondary)

Classification: LCC LB1631 .B391 2019 (print) | LCC LB1631 (ebook) | DDC
428.00712--dc23

Reprinted at Versa Press, July 2020

For a list of corrections, please visit **www.welltrainedmind.com/corrections.**

TABLE OF CONTENTS

PARTS OF SPEECH

"Part of speech" is a term that explains what a word does.

NOUNS

Types of nouns

A noun names a person, place, thing, or idea.

Concrete nouns can be observed with our senses.

      shrimp   tree   gold

Abstract nouns cannot.

      delight   victory   pride

A common noun is a name common to many persons, places, things, or ideas.

      planet

A proper noun is the special, particular name for a person, place, thing, or idea. Proper nouns always begin with capital letters.

      Mars

A collective noun names a group of people, animals, or things.

      family   orchestra   constellation

A compound noun is a single noun composed of two or more words.

One word:	shipwreck, haircut, chalkboard
Hyphenated word:	self-confidence, check-in, pinch-hitter
Two or more words:	air conditioning, North Dakota, *The Prince and the Pauper*

Capitalization rules

1. Capitalize the proper names of persons, places, things, and animals.

      Gandalf   Alderaan   Honda   Lassie

2. Capitalize the names of holidays.

> New Year's Day

3. Capitalize the names of deities.

> Zeus   God   Allah   Great Spirit

4. Capitalize the days of the week and the months of the year, but not the seasons.

> Tuesday   January   winter

5. Capitalize the first, last, and other important words in titles of books, magazines, newspapers, stories, poems, and songs. Italicize the titles of books, magazines, and newspapers. Put the titles of stories, poems, and songs into quotation marks.

> *Alice's Adventures in Wonderland*   "Casey At the Bat"

6. Capitalize and italicize the first, last, and other important words in the names of ships, trains, and planes.

> *Titanic*   *The Orient Express*   *The Spirit of St. Louis*

Gender

Nouns have gender.

Nouns can be masculine, feminine, or neuter.

We use "neuter" for nouns that have no gender, or for nouns whose gender is unknown.

> masculine   bull
> feminine   cow
> neuter   calf

Plural formation

1. Usually, add -s to a noun to form the plural.

> desk   desks

2. Add -es to nouns ending in -s, -sh, -ch, -x, or -z.

> mess   messes

3. If a noun ends in -y after a consonant, change the y to i and add -es.

> family   families

4. If a noun ends in -*y* after a vowel, just add -*s*.

   toy   toys

5. Words ending in -*f*, -*fe*, or -*ff* form their plurals differently.

   5a. For words that end in -*f* or -*fe*, change the *f* or *fe* to *v* and add -*es*.

      leaf   leaves

   5b. For words that end in -*ff*, simply add -*s*.

      sheriff   sheriffs

   5c. Some words that end in a single -*f* can form their plurals either way.

      scarf   scarfs
                       scarves

6. If a noun ends in -*o* after a vowel, just add -*s*.

   patio   patios

7. If a noun ends in -*o* after a consonant, form the plural by adding -*es*.

   potato   potatoes

8. To form the plural of foreign words ending in -*o*, just add -*s*.

   piano   pianos

9. Irregular plurals don't follow any of these rules.

   child   children
   foot   feet
   mouse   mice
   fish   fish

10. Compound nouns are pluralized in different ways.

   10a. If a compound noun is made up of one noun along with another word or words, pluralize the noun.

      brother-in-law   brothers-in-law

   10b. If a compound noun ends in -*ful*, pluralize by putting an -*s* at the end of the entire word.

      truckful   truckfuls

   10c. If neither element of the compound noun is a noun, pluralize the entire word.

      grown-up   grown-ups

10d. If the compound noun includes more than one noun, choose the most important to pluralize.

secretary of state   secretaries of state

Noun "imposters"

A gerund is a present participle acting as a noun.

gerund (object of the preposition)
I have never developed indigestion from **eating** my words.

Winston Churchill

A noun clause takes the place of a noun. Noun clauses can be introduced by relative pronouns, relative adverbs, or subordinating conjunctions. *See "noun clauses," p. 58.*

noun clause serving as direct object
How do the Wise know **that this ring is his**?

J. R. R. Tolkien, *The Fellowship of the Ring*

Nouns that can serve as other parts of speech

Numbers can serve as either nouns or adjectives.

Cardinal numbers represent quantities (one, two, three, four . . .). They can be either nouns or adjectives.

noun
One of these papers was a letter to this girl Agnes, and the other a will.

adjective
The housebreaker freed **one** arm, and grasped his pistol.

Charles Dickens, *Oliver Twist*

Ordinal numbers represent order (first, second, third, fourth . . .). They can be either nouns or adjectives.

Then, at a grocer's shop, we bought an egg and a slice of streaky bacon;
noun
which still left what I thought a good deal of change, out of the **second** of the bright shillings, and made me consider London a very cheap place.

adjective
My mother had a sure foreboding at the **second** glance, that it was Miss Betsey.

Charles Dickens, *David Copperfield*

An adverbial noun tells the time or place of an action, or explains how long, how far, how deep, how thick, or how much. It can modify a verb,

adjective or adverb. **An adverbial noun plus its modifiers is an adverbial noun phrase.**

> The manure should be cleaned out **morning**, **noon**, and again at night.
> "The Horse and His Treatment"

ADJECTIVES

An adjective modifies a noun or pronoun.
Adjectives tell what kind, which one, how many, and whose.

An adjective that comes right before the noun it modifies is in the *attributive position*.
An adjective that follows the noun is in the *predicative position*.

Descriptive adjectives tell what kind.
> **A descriptive adjective becomes an abstract noun when you add *-ness* to it.**
> **The past participle of a verb can act as a descriptive adjective.**
> **The present participle of a verb can act as a descriptive adjective.**

descriptive
attributive position
The cold within him froze his **old** features, nipped his pointed nose,

descriptive
predictive position
shrivelled his cheek, stiffened his gait; made his eyes **red**, his thin lips

descriptive   descriptive
predicative position   present participle
blue; and spoke out shrewdly in his **grating** voice.

descriptive adjective
past participle
descriptive adjective
Quiet and **dark**, beside him stood the Phantom, with its **outstretched** hand.

abstract noun
Darkness is cheap, and Scrooge liked it.
> Charles Dickens, *A Christmas Carol*

Articles modify nouns and answer the question "which one."
The articles are a, an, and the.

> **Use *a* to modify a nonspecific noun that begins with a consonant and *an* to modify a nonspecific noun that begins with a vowel. Use *the* to modify specific nouns.**

> Go on in **the** house and wash up, Gabe . . . I'll fix you **a s**andwich.

> You're **a d**ay late and **a d**ollar short when it comes to **an u**nderstanding with me.
> August Wilson, *Fences*

Demonstrative adjectives modify nouns and answer the question "which one."

    this, that, these, those

Demonstrative pronouns demonstrate or point out something. They take the place of a single word or a group of words.

demonstrative pronoun
These are the seven entrances to the home under the ground, for which
                    demonstrative adjective
Hook has been searching in vain **these** many moons.

J. M. Barrie, Peter Pan

Indefinite adjectives modify nouns and answer the questions "which one" and "how many."

Singular indefinite adjectives:
another   other   one
either   neither   each
Plural indefinite adjectives:
both   few   many   several
Singular or plural indefinite adjectives:
all   any   most   no   some   enough   much

    singular indefinite adjective modifies singular noun "attention"
I do not think that nearly **enough** attention is being given to the possibility of another attack from the Martians.

H. G. Wells, The War of the Worlds

This violates a basic principle of numbers called the axiom of
               plural indefinite adjective modifies plural noun "times"
Archimedes, which says that if you add something to itself **enough** times, it will exceed any other number in magnitude.

Charles Seife, Zero: The Biography of a Dangerous Idea

            indefinite pronoun acting as direct object
On the day before Thanksgiving she would have just **enough** to pay the remaining $4.

O. Henry, "The Purple Dress"

Interrogative adjectives modify nouns and answer the questions "which one" and "how many."

    who, whom, whose, what, which

Interrogative pronouns take the place of nouns in questions.

The interrogative words who, whom, whose, what, and which can also serve as relative pronouns in adjective clauses or introductory words in noun clauses.

interrogative adjective (modifies "sort")   interrogative adjective (modifies "kind")
What sort of place had I come to, and among **what** kind of people?
interrogative pronoun (direct object of "could do")
What could I do but bow acceptance?

introductory word in noun clause
(clause is direct object of "know")
Do you know where you are going, and **what** you are going to?
Bram Stoker, *Dracula*

Possessive adjectives tell whose.

An apostrophe is a punctuation mark that shows possession. It turns a noun into an adjective that tells whose [possessive adjective].

Form the possessive of a singular noun by adding an apostrophe and the letter s.

Rurik's   goose's   airplane's

Form the possessive of a plural noun ending in -s by adding an apostrophe only.

girls'   chickens'   airplanes'

Form the possessive of a plural noun that does not end in -s as if it were a singular noun.

men's   geese's

Possessive personal pronouns show possession and act as adjectives.

my, mine, our, ours, your, yours, his, her, hers, its, their, theirs

Attributive Form	*Predicative Form*
my	mine
your	yours
his, her, its	his, hers, its
our	ours
your	yours
their	theirs

possessive personal pronouns
predicative form
"The Last Doll, indeed!" said Miss Minchin. "And she is **mine**, not **yours**."

possessive personal pronoun
attributive form
"No," said Sara, laughing. "It was **my** rat."

possessive personal pronoun
attributive form
It's a good thing not to answer **your** enemies.
Francis Hodgson Burnett, *A Little Princess*

Appositive adjectives directly follow the word they modify.

It was a spot **remote, sequestered, cloistered** from the business and pleasures of the world.
Edward Bulwer-Lytton, *Alice: The Mysteries*

A proper adjective is formed from a proper name. Proper adjectives are capitalized.

He arrived at the Old Vic determined to do away with the old-fashioned actor-manager type of **Shakespearean** production that dated from the **Victorian** era.
Piers Paul Read, *Alec Guinness: The Authorised Biography*

Words that are not usually capitalized remain lower-case even when they are attached to a proper adjective.

The *Mayflower* carried the **anti-Christmas** sentiment of the Puritans with it across the Atlantic, so the holiday took a long time to take hold in the New World.
Michael Judge, *The Dance of Time*

A compound adjective combines two words into a single adjective with a single meaning.
Compound adjectives answer the questions "what kind" and "how many."
Hyphens connect compound adjectives in the attributive position. Compound adjectives in the predicative position are not usually hyphenated.

It is the natural order of things for virtuous men to create a faction with other virtuous men because they share the same way, and for **narrow-minded** men to create factions with other **narrow-minded** men because of gain.

Ouyang Xiu

Pih-e was **narrow minded**, and Lew-hea Hwuy was deficient in gravity; therefore, the superior man follows neither of them.

Mencius

A predicate adjective describes the subject and is found in the complete predicate.

All emotions, and that one particularly, were **abhorrent** to his cold, precise but admirably balanced mind.
> A. Conan Doyle, "A Scandal in Bohemia"

The positive degree of an adjective describes only one thing.

It is a **good** thing.

The comparative degree of an adjective compares two things.

It is a far, far **better** thing that I do, than I have ever done.
> Charles Dickens, *A Tale of Two Cities*

The superlative degree of an adjective compares three or more things.

It was the **best** of times, it was the **worst** of times.
> Charles Dickens, *A Tale of Two Cities*

Spelling Rules for Forming Comparatives and Superlatives
Most regular adjectives form the comparative by adding -r or -er.
Most regular adjectives form the superlative by adding -st or -est.

If the adjective ends in -e already, add only -r or -st.

noble   nobler   noblest

If the adjective ends in a short vowel sound and a consonant, double the consonant and add -er or -est.

red   redder   reddest

If the adjective ends in -y, change the y to i and add -er or -est.

hazy   hazier   haziest

Many adjectives form their comparative and superlative forms by adding the word *more* or *most* before the adjective instead of using -er or -est.

unusual   more unusual   most unusual

In comparative and superlative adjective forms, the words *more* and *most* are used as adverbs.

Irregular adjectives form the comparative and superlative by changing form.

good   better   best
bad   worse   worst

Do not use *more* with an adjective or adverb that is already in the comparative form.

He is ~~more~~ hungrier than you are.

Do not use *most* with an adjective or adverb that is already in the superlative form.

That's the ~~most~~ reddest sunset I've ever seen.

Use an adjective form when an adjective is needed and an adverb form when an adverb is needed.

superlative adjective modifying the noun "time"
The steps must be taken in the **quickest** time.
Irving Brokaw, *The Art of Skating*

The skater will quickly find out for himself how the straps

superlative adverb
modifying "can be adjusted"
can be **most quickly** and comfortably adjusted.
T. Maxwell Witham, *Figure-Skating*

An adjective clause is a dependent clause that acts as an adjective in a sentence, modifying a noun or pronoun in the independent clause.

Relative pronouns introduce adjective clauses and refer back to an antecedent in the independent clause.

who, whom, whose, which, that.

relative pronoun refers back to antecedent "order"
Speak to me of the religious order **whose chief you are.**
Alexandre Dumas, *The Man in the Iron Mask*

***Who* always acts as a subject or predicate nominative within a sentence or clause. *Whom* always acts as an object.**

It was Phileas Fogg, whose head now emerged from behind
subject of the underlined adjective clause
his newspapers, **who** <u>made this remark</u>.

object of
the preposition
You forget that it is I with **whom** you have to deal, sir; for it
direct object of the
underlined adjective clause
was I **whom** <u>you not only insulted, but struck</u>!
Jules Verne, *Around the World in Eighty Days*

The interrogative words who, whom, whose, what, and which can also serve as relative pronouns in adjective clauses or introductory words in noun clauses.

noun clause   noun clause   adjective clause with relative
acting as subject   acting as appositive   pronoun ("it" is antecedent)

What was it—I paused to think—**what** was it <u>that</u> <u>so unnerved</u>
<u>me</u> in the contemplation of the House of Usher?

Edgar Allan Poe, *The Fall of the House of Usher*

Adjective clauses can be introduced by prepositions.

They were coming to a thicket of juniper and dog roses, tangled at

adjective clause introduced by preposition "on" modifies "trails"

ground level with nettles and trails of bryony **on which the berries**
were now beginning to ripen and turn red.

Richard Adams, *Watership Down*

Adjective clauses should usually go immediately before or after the
noun or pronoun they modify.

correct placement (bolded clause modifies "truck")

He stumbled his way to the <u>truck</u> **that was parked at an angle** near
the tall, flashing neon sign.

Mark Rashid, *Out of the Wild*

A restrictive modifying clause defines the word that it modifies.
Removing the clause changes the essential meaning of the sentence.

A nonrestrictive modifying clause describes the word that it modifies.
Removing the clause doesn't change the essential meaning of the
sentence.

Only nonrestrictive clauses should be set off by commas.

restrictive adjective clause

The elaborate machinery **which was once used to make men**
responsible is now used solely in order to shift the responsibility.

nonrestrictive adjective clause

This idea, **which is the core of ethics,** is the core of the nursery-tales.

G. K. Chesterton, *All Things Considered*

Traditionally, when the relative pronoun introducting a modifying
clause refers to a thing rather than a person, "which" introduces
nonrestrictive clauses and "that" introduces restrictive clauses. (This
rule is no longer universally observed; see the examples above)

nonrestrictive

The feast of Tara was held, **at which all were gathered together.**

restrictive

She was singing lullabies to a cat **that was yelping on her shoulder.**

James Stephens, *Irish Fairy Tales*

Descriptive adjectives *describe* by giving additional details.
Limiting adjectives *define* by setting limits.

Descriptive Adjectives	Limiting Adjectives
Regular	Possessives
Present participles	Articles
Past participles	Demonstratives
	Indefinites
	Interrogatives
	Numbers

Cardinal numbers represent quantities (one, two, three, four . . .). They can be either nouns or adjectives.
Ordinal numbers represent order (first, second, third, fourth . . .). They can be either nouns or adjectives.
See nouns, p. 4.

Use "fewer" for concrete items and "less" for abstractions.

concrete
Her attainments were **fewer** than were usually possessed by girls of her age and station.

Charlotte Bronte, *Shirley*

abstract
With little ceremony, and **less** courtesy, he pointed out what he termed her errors.

Charlotte Bronte, *Villette*

A misplaced modifier is an adjective, adjective phrase, adverb, or adverb phrase in the wrong place.

INCORRECT: Lost: A cow belonging to an old woman **with brass knobs on her horns**.
CORRECT: Lost: A cow **with brass knobs on her horns,** belonging to an old woman.

A squinting modifier can belong either to the sentence element preceding or the element following.

INCORRECT: Children who watch TV **rarely** turn out to be readers.
CORRECT: Children who **rarely** watch TV turn out to be readers.
CORRECT: **Rarely,** children who watch TV turn out to be readers.

A dangling modifier has no noun or verb to modify.

INCORRECT: **Tearing open the envelope**, a thick wad of bills fell out.

CORRECT: Tearing open the envelope, the blackmailer found a thick wad of bills.
CORRECT: As the blackmailer tore open the envelope, a thick wad of bills fell out.

Comparisons can be formed using a combination of *more* and *fewer* or *less;* a combination of *more* and *more* or *fewer/less* and *fewer/less*; a combination of *more* or *fewer/less* with a comparative form; or simply two comparative forms.

In comparisons using *more . . . fewer* and *more . . . less, more* and *less* can act as either adverbs or adjectives and *the* can act as an adverb.

adjective

He would do very well if he had **fewer** cakes and sweetmeats sent him from home.

adverb

I wanted to tease you a little to make you **less** sad.

Charlotte Bronte, *Jane Eyre*

When *than* is used in a comparison and introduces a clause with understood elements, it is acting as a subordinating conjunction.

He gave one the idea that he had been active **rather than** [that he had been] strong; his shoulders were not broad for his height, though certainly not narrow.

Charles Darwin, *The Life and Letters of Charles Darwin*

***More than* and *less than* are compound modifiers.**

compound adverb

How much **more than** delightful to go to some good concert or fine opera.

Charles Darwin, *The Life and Letters of Charles Darwin*

An adjective of negation (*no*) states what is not true or does not exist.

Do not use two adverbs or adjectives of negation together.

INCORRECT: I have**n't** heard **no** good of such folk.
CORRECT: I have heard **no** good of such folk.
CORRECT: I have**n't** heard good of such folk.

PRONOUNS

A pronoun takes the place of a noun.
The antecedent is the noun that is replaced by the pronoun.

pronoun without   pronoun replacing
antecedent   antecedent "driver"

The driver saw **it** at the same moment; **he** at once checked the horses, and, jumping to the ground, disappeared into the darkness.

Bram Stoker, Dracula

Personal Pronouns

	Singular	**Plural**
First person:	I, me, my, mine	we, us, our, ours
Second person:	you, your, yours	you, your, yours
Third person:	he, she, it, him, her, his, hers, its	they, them, their, theirs

Object personal pronouns are used as objects in sentences.

me, you, him, her, it, us, them

Subject personal pronouns are used as subjects and predicate nominatives in sentences.

I, you, he, she, it, we, they

subject of   subject of
adjective clause   sentence

Wondering what bargain **we** had made, **I** turned to the class for an

object of preposition

answer, but the class looked back at **me** in puzzlement.

Harper Lee, To Kill a Mockingbird

Possessive personal pronouns show possession and act as adjectives.

my, mine, our, ours, your, yours, his, hers, its, their, theirs

See possessive adjectives, p. 7

Indefinite pronouns are pronouns without antecedents.

Singular:

anybody	anyone	anything
everybody	everyone	everything
nobody	no one	nothing
somebody	someone	something
another	other	one
either	neither	each

Plural:

both	few	many	several

Singular or Plural:

all	any	most	none	some

Nobody under the bed; **nobody** in the closet; **nobody** in his dressing-gown, which was hanging up in a suspicious attitude against the wall.
Charles Dickens, *A Christmas Carol*

For indefinite adjectives, see p. 6

Reflexive and intensive pronouns combine -self or -selves with personal pronouns.

Reflexive pronouns refer back to the subject.

The widow rocked **herself** to and fro, and wrung her hands.
Charles Dickens, *The Pickwick Papers*

Intensive pronouns emphasize a noun or another pronoun.

The old lady **herself** laughed very heartily indeed.
Charles Dickens, *The Pickwick Papers*

Do NOT use theirselves, hisself, or ourself.

Demonstrative pronouns demonstrate or point out something. They take the place of a single word or a group of words.

this, that, these, those

There is a tender regard one woman bears to another, and a natural sympathy in **those** that have gone thro' the Pangs of Childbearing.
Laurel Thatcher Ulrich, *A Midwife's Tale*

Demonstrative adjectives modify nouns and answer the question "which one."
See demonstrative adjectives, p. 6.

Interrogative pronouns take the place of nouns in questions.

who, whom, whose, what, which

But **what** shall we call the women?
Laurel Thatcher Ulrich, *A Midwife's Tale*

Interrogative adjectives modify nouns and answer the questions "which one" and "how many."

Who **always acts as a subject or predicate nominative within a sentence or clause.** *Whom* **always acts as an object.**

direct object
"What victim?" said Judge Obadiah. "Burn **whom**? In Bombay itself?"

subject
"**Who** knows?" replied Mr. Fogg, returning to the car as coolly as usual.

Jules Verne, *Around the World in Eighty Days*

VERBS

Basics

A verb shows an action, shows a state of being, links two words together, or helps another verb.

Persons of the Verb

	Singular	Plural
First person:	I	we
Second person:	you	you
Third person:	he, she, it (singular nouns)	they (plural nouns)

A state of being verb expresses existence.

Am, is, are, was, were, be, being, been

State of being verbs do not have voice.

In himself he **is**.

William Shakespeare, *A Midsummer's Night Dream*

A linking verb connects the subject to a noun, pronoun, or adjective in the complete predicate.
A predicate adjective describes the subject and is found in the complete predicate.
A predicate nominative renames the subject and is found in the complete predicate.

linking   predicate   predicate   predicate
subject verb   adjective   adjective   adjective

He was quite **young**, wonderfully **handsome**, extremely **agreeable**, and to crown the whole, he meant to be at the next assembly with a large party.

linking   predicate
subject verb   nominative

She was a **woman** of mean understanding, little information, and uncertain temper.

Jane Austen, *Pride & Prejudice*

State of Being/Linking Verbs

am, is, are, was, were
be, being, been

Linking Verbs That Can Also Be Action Verbs

taste, feel, smell, sound, look
prove, grow,
remain, appear, stay
become, seem

       action verb   direct object
Mr. Darcy **felt** their rudeness and immediately said, "This walk is not wide enough for our party. We had better go into the avenue."

linking   predicate   predicate
  verb   adjective   adjective
I **felt** a little uneasy—a little fearful of my sister's happiness with him in marriage, because I knew that his conduct had not been always quite right.

                                 Jane Austen, *Pride & Prejudice*

A helping verb helps the main verb to express its meaning.
A verb phrase is the main verb plus any helping verbs.

Helping Verbs

Am, is, are, was, were
Be, being, been
Have, has, had
Do, does, did
Shall, will, should, would, may, might, must
Can, could

          verb phrase
   It **would have been hurt** just the same whether we'd been rowing or not.
      helping verbs   main verb

Use the helping verbs *do, does,* and *did* to form negatives, ask questions, and provide emphasis.

negative	I **do** not **want** you to give me anything.
question	**Do** you **think** you could walk if we helped you?
question	Whatever on earth **does** that **mean**?
emphasis	Hearing about blood and wounds **does** really **make** me feel most awfully funny.
emphasis	Those men last night **did bring** very bad news.
question	And what **did** she **say**?

                              E. Nesbit, *The Railway Children*

When three or more nouns, adjectives, verbs, or adverbs appear in a series, they should be separated by commas.

All action verbs have mood, voice, and tense.
State of being verbs have only mood and tense.

Mood

Indicative verbs affirm or declare what actually is. Indicative verbs express real actions.

>   indicative (action)   indicative (action)
> The socket from which the dragon's crest <u>had been torn</u> <u>was lined</u> with
>   indicative (action)
> flat stones, and in it, as in a narrow grave, <u>lay</u> Dyrnwyn, the black
> sword.

Modal verbs express situations that have not actually happpened. Modal verbs express possible actions.

Subjunctive verbs express situations that are unreal, wished for, or uncertain. Subjunctive verbs express unreal actions.

>   subjunctive (action)   modal (state of being)
> If any life <u>be staked</u> against Arawn Death-Lord, it <u>must be</u> mine.

>   indicative (action)
> Huge blocks of ice <u>thundered</u> down the slope, bounding and rolling as if

>   subjunctive (state of being)
> they <u>had been</u> no more than pebbles.

Imperative verbs express intended actions.

>   indicative (action)   imperative (action)
> You <u>have learned</u> much, but <u>learn</u> this last and hardest of lessons.
>   Lloyd Alexander, *The High King*

Voice

Active voice: In a sentence with an active verb, the subject performs the action.
Passive voice: In a sentence with a passive verb, the subject receives the action.

<u>ACTIVE:</u>	<u>PASSIVE:</u>
Simple present:	**am/is/are + past participle**
Freddy tricks the alligator.	The alligator is tricked by Freddy.
Simple past:	**was/were + past participle**
Freddy tricked the alligator.	The alligator was tricked by Freddy.
Simple future:	**will be + past participle**
Freddy will trick the alligator.	The alligator will be tricked by Freddy.

Progressive present:	**is/are being + past participle**
Freddy is tricking the alligator.	The alligator is being tricked by Freddy.
Progressive past:	**was/were being + past participle**
Freddy was tricking the alligator.	The alligator was being tricked by Freddy.
Progressive future:	***will be being + past participle**
Freddy will be tricking the alligator.	The alligator will be being tricked by Freddy.
Perfect present:	**has/have been + past participle**
Freddy has tricked the alligator.	The alligator has been tricked by Freddy.
Perfect past:	**had been + past participle**
Freddy had tricked the alligator.	The alligator had been tricked by Freddy.
Perfect future:	**will have been + past participle**
Freddy will have tricked the alligator.	The alligator will have been tricked by Freddy.
Progressive perfect past:	**had + been being + past participle**
Freddy had been tricking the alligator.	The alligator had been being tricked by Freddy.
Progressive perfect present:	**has/have + been being + past participle**
Freddy has been tricking the alligator.	The alligator has been being tricked by Freddy.
Progressive perfect future:	***will have been being + past participle**
Freddy will have been tricking the alligator.	The alligator will have been being tricked by Freddy.

*The passive form of progressive future verbs is awkward and not often used.

NOTE: *Shall* and *will* are different forms of the same verb.

Transitive verbs express action that is received by some person or thing. Intransitive verbs express action that is not received by any person or thing.

Common Intransitive Verbs

cough   go   arrive

Common Transitive Verbs

love   eat   help

Ambitransitive verbs can be either transitive or intransitive.

Verbs That Can Be Used As Transitive or Intransitive

taste   eat   sing

  transitive   The horse eats the apple.
  intransitive   The horse is eating hungrily.

Transitive verbs can be active or passive.
Intransitive verbs can only be active.

Sit, _lie_, and _rise_ are intransitive.

   I will sit quietly during the lecture.
   I will lie upon the daisies and stare at the sky.
   I will rise early in the morning.

Set, _lay_, and _raise_ are transitive.

   I will set my book on the desk during the lecture.
   I will lay a blanket down on the grass before I lie down on it.
   I will raise the window shades as soon as the sun comes up.

Tense

A verb in the present tense tells about something that happens in the present.
A verb in the past tense tells about something that happened in the past.
A verb in the future tense tells about something that will happen in the future.

Verbs in the simple past, simple present, and simple future describe actions that simply happen.

              simple past   simple past
   All day long he <u>flew</u>, and at night-time he <u>arrived</u> at the city.
                     simple present
   The Happy Prince never <u>dreams</u> of crying for anything.
    simple future
   I <u>will wait</u> with you one night longer.
                                  Oscar Wilde, *The Happy Prince*

Form the simple future by adding the helping verb "will" in front of the simple present.

> we finish
> we will finish

Form the simple past by adding the suffix -ed to the simple present
A suffix is one or more letters added to the end of a word to change its meaning.

> we finish
> we finished

If the basic verb ends in e already, only add -*d*.

> we love
> we loved

If the verb ends in a short vowel sound and a consonant, double the consonant and add -*ed*.

> we pat
> we patted

If the verb ends in -y following a consonant, change the -y to -i and add -*ed*.

> they study
> they studied

A progressive verb describes an ongoing or continuous action.
Progressive verbs usually end in -ing.

progressive past

A young man and woman, the latter carrying a child, <u>were approaching</u> the large village of Weydon-Priors, in Upper Wessex, on foot.

progressive present

I <u>am thinking</u> of Mr. Henchard's sudden liking for that young man.

progressive future

You <u>will be standing</u> in view of my house to-day for two or three hours in the course of your business, so do please call and see me.

Thomas Hardy, *The Mayor of Casterbridge*

Spelling Rules for Adding -Ing
If the verb ends in a short vowel sound and a consonant, double the consonant and add -*ing*.

> eat   eating
> run   running

If the verb ends in a consonant and an e, drop the e and add *-ing*.

> rate   rating

The progressive past tense uses the helping verbs *was* and *were*.

> I was eating   they were running

The progressive present tense uses the helping verbs *am*, *is*, and *are*.

> I am running   he is rating   they are running

The progressive future tense uses the helping verbs *will be*.

> I will be eating   they will be eating

A perfect verb describes an action which has been completed before another action takes place.

Perfect past verbs describe an action that was finished in the past before another action began. The perfect past tense uses the helping verb *had*.

> During the Revolution, Hamilton had stuffed Malachy
> Postlethwayt's *Universal Dictionary of Trade and Commerce* into his
> satchel, and now he used it once again.
>   Ron Chernow, *Alexander Hamilton*

Perfect present verbs describe an action that was completed before the present moment. The perfect present tense uses the helping verbs *have* and *has*.

> Slyness and untruthfulness—that's what she has displayed.
>   L. M. Montgomery, *Anne of Green Gables*

Perfect future verbs describe an action that will be finished in the future before another action begins. The perfect future tense uses the helping verb phrase *will have* or *shall have*.

> In another hour and thirty minutes Mercédès will have become
> Madame Dantès.
>   Alexandre Dumas, *The Count of Monte Cristo*

A progressive perfect verb describes an ongoing or continuous action that has a definite end.

progressive perfect past
> (active) I had been running for half an hour before I decided to stop.
> (passive) The house had been being shown to prospective buyers.

progressive perfect present
> (active) I have been running all morning.
> (passive) I have been being sent to the post office by my boss every day.

progressive perfect future
> (active) I will have been running for an hour by the time you arrive.
> (passive) By June, the students will have been being taught Latin for two years.

Irregular verbs form past, present and future tenses by changing form.

eat	ate	will have eaten
become	became	will have become
cast	cast	will have cast
withdraw	withdrew	will have withdrawn

English verbs have three principal parts.

First Principal Part: The Simple Present (Present)   "Present"

(I) conjugate	(I) juggle	(I) become	(I) feel

Second Principal Part: The Simple Past (Past) "Past"

(I) conjugated	(I) juggled	(I) became	(I) felt

Third Principal Part: The Perfect Past, Minus Helping Verbs   "Past Participle"

(I have) conjugated	(I have) juggled	(I) become	(I) felt

SAME PRESENT, PAST & PAST PARTICIPLE

burst	burst	burst
quit	quit	quit
shut	shut	shut

SAME PAST & PAST PARTICIPLE

send	sent	sent
feed	fed	fed
read	read	read
lay	laid	laid

SAME PRESENT AND PAST PARTICIPLE, BUT PAST DIFFERS

become	became	become
come	came	come
run	ran	run

THREE DIFFERENT IRREGULAR FORMS

break	broke	broken
eat	ate	eaten
begin	began	begun
fly	flew	flown
do	did	done
go	went	gone
lie	lay	lain

Troublesome Irregular Verbs:

Verb	Principal Parts	Definition
sit	(sit, sat, sat):	to rest or be seated
set	(set, set, set):	to put or place something
lie	(lie, lay, lain):	to rest or recline
lay	(lay, laid, laid):	to put or place something
rise	(rise, rose, risen):	to get up or go up
raise	(raise, raised, raised):	to cause something to go up or grow up
let	(let, let, let):	to allow
leave	(leave, left, left):	to go away from or allow to remain

The past participle of a verb can act as a descriptive adjective.

The **raised** window let in the fresh air.

The present participle of a verb can act as a descriptive adjective.

The **rising** sun streamed in.

A gerund is a present participle acting as a noun.

Rising early is hard to do.

An infinitive is formed by combining *to* and the first-person singular present form of a verb.

I sing.   I sang.   I love **to sing**.

A passive infinitive is formed by combining *to be* and the past participle of a verb.

The song needs **to be sung**.

Infinitives and infinitive phrases can act as nouns, adjectives, or adverbs.

all three infinitives acting as nouns:
          compound subject

To censure, to depose, or **to punish** with death the first magistrate of the republic, who had abused his delegated trust, was the ancient and undoubted prerogative of the Roman senate.

Edward Gibbon, *The History of the Decline and Fall of the Roman Empire,* Vol. 1

adjective phrase modifying "inability"

The inability of Nanjing **to impose** an effective land tax on the Red river valley had benefits for landowners and tenant farmers alike.

adverb phrase modifying "unable"

"Unable **to attain** his ambition," we are told, "the disappointed
adverb phrase modifying "determined"
candidate went home determined **to improve** his own prospects."

Arthur Cotterell, *A History of Southeast Asia*

Modal verbs express situations that have not actually happened.

Modal verbs are formed with the helping verbs *should, would, may, might, must, can,* and *could.*

would, can, could, may, might: **possibility**

Would there be any way I could travel parallel to the fire and work my way back there, to a source of water at least?

Suzanne Collins, *The Hunger Games*

must, should: **obligation**

Peeta should have gone into his private session with the Gamemakers and painted himself into a tree.

Suzanne Collins, *The Hunger Games*

may: **permission**

Finally he clears his throat and says, "You may go now now, Miss Everdeen."

Suzanne Collins, *Catching Fire*

can: **ability**

You can tell it was built for a larger gathering, and perhaps it held one before the pox epidemic.

Suzanne Collins, *Mockingjay*

Modal Tense Formation
Simple Present

active	I can help	modal helping verb + first person singular
passive	I should be helped	modal helping verb + be + past participle

Progressive Present

active	I might be helping	modal helping verb + be + present participle
passive	I could be being helped	modal helping verb + be + being + past participle

Perfect Present

active	I would have helped	modal helping verb + have + past participle
passive	I may have been helped	modal helping verb + have + been + past participle

Progressive Perfect Present

active	I must have been helping	modal helping verb + have + been + present participle
passive	I could have been being helped	modal helping verb + have + been + being + past participle

Modal Tense

	Simple Present	Simple Past	Simple Future
active	I should help	*none*	*none*
passive	I should be helped	*none*	*none*

	Progressive Present	Progressive Past	Progressive Future
active	I could be helping	*none*	*none*
passive	I could be being helped	*none*	*none*

	Perfect Present	Perfect Past	Perfect Future
active	I would have helped	*none*	*none*
passive	I would have been helped	*none*	*none*

Progressive Perfect Present		Progressive Perfect Past	Progressive Perfect Future
active	I might have been helping	*none*	*none*
passive	I might have been being helped	*none*	*none*

Use the simple present modal or progressive present modal when the situation isn't happening in the present.

simple present modal, action
If we **could**, somehow, **get** a vote of the people of Tennessee and have

simple present modal, state of being
it result properly, it **would be** worth more to us than a battle gained.
Abraham Lincoln, *Collected Works, Vol. 5*

Use the perfect present modal or the progressive perfect present modal when the situation didn't happen in the past.

perfect present modal, action
Yet Lincoln, had he desired, **could have** easily **moved** back to Kentucky like his friend Joshua Speed and, with the support of his prominent father-in-law, established himself as a member of Lexington's slaveowning high society. He chose not to do so.
Eric Foner, *The Fiery Trial: Abraham Lincoln and American Slavery*

Use the helping verbs *do, does,* and *did* to form negatives, ask questions, and provide emphasis.

negative verb
Machines **do** not **have** feelings.

question (and negative verb)
If, for example, you ate the fish with the salad fork, why **did** you not **have** the fish fork left, with which to eat the salad? Miss Manners is always ready to receive back a sinner, but not those who steal the forks.

question
Did you **get** so upset that you walked into a wall?

negative verb
Miss Manners **does** not **believe** in cutting off a symbolic show of
emphasis
affection on the grounds of age. But she **does consider** that childhood is sufficient time for gratitude and reciprocal affection to develop if it is ever going to do so.
Judith Martin, *Miss Manners' Guide to Excruciatingly Correct Behavior*

	first person		*third person*	
simple present	I do believe.	*I believe.*	He does believe.	*He believes.*
simple past	I did believe.	*I believed.*	He did believe.	*He believed.*

Subjunctive verbs express situations that are unreal, wished for, or uncertain. Subjunctive verbs express unreal actions.

If I **were** a swan, I'd be gone.
If I **were** a train, I'd be late again.
And if I **were** a good man, I'd talk with you more often than I do.

Roger Waters, "If"

Indicative Simple Present *Action*		*Subjunctive Simple Present* *Action*	
3rd he, she, it leaves	they leave	he, she, it leave	they leave

Indicative Simple Past *State of Being*		*Subjunctive Simple Past* *State of Being*	
1st I was	we were	I were	we were
3rd he, she, it was	they were	he, she, it were	they were

Indicative Present (Simple) *State of Being*		*Subjunctive Present (Simple)* *State of Being*	
1st I am	we are	I be	we be
2nd you are	you are	you be	you be
3rd he, she, it is	they are	he, she, it be	they be

The present passive subjunctive is formed by pairing *be* with the *past participle* of a verb.

If you **be provoked** with evil-speaking, arm yourself with patience, lenity, and silence.

Certain Sermons or Homilies Appointed to be
Read in Churches in the Time of the Late
Queen Elizabeth of Famous Memory

The present imperative is the first person singular form of the verb with no subject.

The present passive imperative is formed by adding the helping verb *be* to the past participle of the verb.

present passive imperative   present imperative
Yet let us not **be discouraged**, but let us continually **cry** and **call** upon God.

Certain Sermons or Homilies Appointed to be
Read in Churches in the Time of the Late
Queen Elizabeth of Famous Memory

Tense formation summary, action verbs

Indicative Tense	Active formation	Examples	Passive formation	Examples
Simple present	Add -s in 3rd person singular	I confuse he, she, it confuses	am/is/are + past participle	I am confused you are confused he, she, it is confused
Simple past	Add -d or -ed, or change form	I confused	was/were + past participle	I was confused you were confused
Simple future	+ will OR shall	they will confuse	will be + past participle	it will be confused

Progressive present	am/is/are + present participle	I am confusing you are confusing he, she, it is confusing	am/is/are being + past participle	I am being confused you are being confused he, she, it is being confused
Progressive past	was/were + present participle	I was confusing you were confusing	was/were being + past participle	I was being confused you were being confused
Progressive future	will be + present participle	I will be confusing	will be being + past participle	it will be being confused

Indicative Tense	Active formation	Examples	Passive formation	Examples
Perfect present	has/have + past participle	I have confused it has confused	has/have been + past participle	I have been confused it has been confused
Perfect past	had + past participle	they had confused	had been + past participle	you had been confused
Perfect future	will have + past participle	we will have confused	will have been + past participle	they will have been confused

Progressive perfect present	have/has been + present participle	I have been confusing he, she, it has been confusing	have/has been being + past participle	I have been being confused he, she, it has been being confused
Progressive perfect past	had been + present participle	you had been confusing	had been being + past participle	you had been being confused
Progressive perfect future	will have been + present participle	you will have been confusing	will have been being + past participle	they will have been being confused

Modal Tense	Active formation	Examples	Passive formation	Examples
Simple present	modal helping verb + simple present main verb	I could match you should match he, she, it might match	modal helping verb + be + past participle	I can be matched they may be matched
Progressive present	modal helping verb + be + present participle	I could be matching	modal helping verb + be + being + past participle	it might be being matched
Perfect present	modal helping verb + have + past participle	you should have matched	modal helping verb + have + been + past participle	we could have been matched
Progressive perfect present	modal helping verb + have been + present participle	I must have been matching	modal helping verb + have been being + past participle	we must have been being matched

Imperative tense	Active formation	Examples	Passive formation	Examples
Present	Simple present form without subject	Count!	be + past participle	Be counted!

Subjunctive tense	Active formation	Examples	Passive formation	Examples
Simple present	No change in any person	I fear you fear he, she, it fear we fear you fear they fear	be + past participle	I be feared it be feared you be feared
Simple past	**Same as indicative:** Add -d or -ed, or change form	I feared you feared he, she, it feared	were + past participle	he were feared you were feared

Progressive present	**Same as indicative:** am/is/are + present participle	I am fearing you are fearing he, she, it is fearing	**Same as indicative:** am/is/are being + past participle	I am being feared you are being feared he, she, it is being feared

Subjunctive tense	Active formation	Examples	Passive formation	Examples
Progressive past	were + present participle	I were fearing you were fearing he, she, it were fearing	were being + past participle	I were being feared you were being feared he, she, it were being feared
Perfect present	**Same as indicative:** has/have + past participle	I have feared he, she, it has feared they have feared	**Same as indicative:** has/have been + past participle	I have been feared he, she, it has been feared they have been feared
Perfect past	**Same as indicative:** had + past participle	we had feared	**Same as indicative:** had been + past participle	we had been feared

Progressive perfect present	**Same as indicative:** have/has been + present participle	I have been fearing you have been fearing he, she, it has been fearing	**Same as indicative:** have/has been being + past participle	I have been being feared you have been being feared he, she, it has been being feared

Subjunctive tense	Active formation	Examples	Passive formation	Examples
Progressive perfect past	**Same as indicative:** had been + present participle	you had been fearing	**Same as indicative:** had been being + past participle	you had been being feared

A hortative verb encourages or recommends an action.

In first person plural hortative verbs, the helping verb "let" is used.
The state of being verb takes the form "be."
The active verb is the same form as the present active indicative.
The passive verb combines "be" with the past participle.

> Let's be more careful next time.
> Let's run faster.
> Let's be finished now.

In second person hortative verbs, the helping verb "may" is used.
The state of being verb takes the form "be."
The active verb is the same form as the present active indicative.
The passive verb combines "be" with the past participle.

> May you be happy.
> May you walk in joy.
> May you be saved from your own foolishness.

Third person hortative verbs use the helping verbs "let" or "may."
The state of being verb takes the form "be."
The active verb is the same form as the present active subjunctive.
The passive verb combines "be" with the past participle.

> Let the trumpets be sounded.
> May no creature on earth be silent.
> Let the Lord of the Black Lands come forth!

ADVERBS

An adverb modifies a verb, an adjective, or another adverb.

Adverbs tell how, when, where, how often, and to what extent.

adverb modifying verb
and telling when

I had come to cooking **late** in life, and knew from firsthand experience

adverb modifying adjective   adverb modifying adjective
and telling to what extent   and telling how

how frustrating it could be to try to learn from **badly** written recipes.

Julia Child, *My Life in France*

Here and *there* **are adverbs that tell where.**

adverb modifying verb "enter"

We **here** enter upon one of the most interesting and important chapters in the history of music.

W. S. B. Mathews, *A Popular History of the Art of Music*

The positive degree of an adverb describes only one verb, adjective, or adverb.

The comparative degree of an adverb compares two verbs, adjectives, or adverbs.

The superlative degree of an adverb compares three or more verbs, adjectives, or adverbs.

If the adverb ends in –y, change the y to i and add –er or –est.

Most adverbs that end in –ly form their comparative and superlative forms by adding the word *more* or *most* before the adverb instead of using –er or –est.

thoughtfully	more thoughtfully	most thoughtfully
early	earlier	earliest

The Persians wanted to force the passage between Euboea and the main, for the double purpose of safer navigation, and of attending

comparative adverb

more closely the motions of their army.

The Greeks had appropriated all that valuable part of the African coast

superlative adverb

which, after the powerful kingdom of Egypt, lay **nearest** to the Phoenician shore.

William Mitford, *The History of Greece*

Irregular adverbs form the comparative and superlative by changing form.

well	better	best

Do not use *more* with an adjective or adverb that is already in the comparative form.

Do not use *most* with an adjective or adverb that is already in the superlative form.

Use an adjective form when an adjective is needed and an adverb form when an adverb is needed.

When three or more nouns, adjectives, verbs, or adverbs appear in a series, they should be separated by commas.

Adverb clauses modify verbs, adjectives, and other adverbs in the independent clause. They answer the questions where, when, how, how often, and to what extent.

adverb clause introduced by subordinating conjunction
and modifying main verb "realized"

The Glass Cat, **although it had some disagreeable ways and manners**, nevertheless realized that Trot and Cap'n Bill were its friends.

L. Frank Baum, *The Magic of Oz*

Adverb clauses can be introduced by adverbs.

> as and its compounds (as if, as soon as, as though)
> how and its compound (however)
> when and its compound (whenever)
> whence
> where and its compounds (whereat, whereby, wherein, wherefore, whereon)
> while
> whither

Brome sighed and voiced aloud the thought that tormented him

adverb clause modifying verb "tormented"

constantly, **whenever he looked out over the deep waters of the main**.

Brian Jacques, *Martin the Warrior*

Relative adverbs introduce adjective clauses and refer back to a place, time, or reason in the independent clause.

> where, when, why

relative adverb refers back to "interval"

There was a considerable interval **when nobeast was on the walltop**, and she took advantage of this to sneak up to the fortress.

Brian Jacques, *Martin the Warrior*

Subordinating conjunctions and subordinating correlative conjunctions often join an adverb clause to an independent clause.

> **Adverbs can act as subordinating conjunctions when they connect adverb clauses to a verb, adjective, or adverb in the main clause.**

> after
> although

as (as soon as)
because
before
if
in order that
lest
since
though
till
unless
until
although/though . . . yet/still
if . . . then

adverb clause modifying main verb

She possibly might never be fully handsome, <u>**unless** the carking</u>

adverb clause modifying verb of previous clause

<u>accidents of her daily existence could be evaded **before** the</u>
<u>mobile parts of her countenance had settled to their final mould</u>.

Thomas Hardy, The Mayor of Casterbridge

When *than* is used in a comparison and introduces a clause with understood elements, it is acting as a subordinating conjunction.

Considering that there is no natural boundary between the two places, and that the character of the country is nearly similar, the difference was much greater **than I should have expected [it to be]**.

Charles Darwin, The Voyage of the Beagle

A misplaced modifier is an adjective, adjective phrase, adverb, or adverb phrase in the wrong place.

adverb phrase "without pain" should follow the verb "consider";
misplaced, it becomes an adjective phrase modifying "you"

I can't even consider leaving you **without pain.**

A squinting modifier can belong either to the sentence element preceding or the element following.

unclear whether the adverb modifies "watch" or "turn out"

Children who watch TV **rarely** turn out to be readers.

A dangling modifier has no noun or verb to modify.

After pointing out my errors, I was sent out of the room.

Comparisons can be formed using a combination of *more* and *fewer* or *less*; a combination of *more* and *more* or *fewer/less* and *fewer/less*; a

combination of *more* or *fewer/less* with a comparative form; or simply two comparative forms.

> In comparisons using *more . . . fewer* and *more . . . less, more* and *less* can act as either adverbs or adjectives and *the* can act as an adverb.

<table>
<tr><td>adverb
modifying
"longer"</td><td>adverb
modifying
"live"</td><td>adverb
modifying
"more"</td><td>adverb
modifying
"widens"</td><td>adverb
modifying
"less"</td><td>adverb
modifying
"prone"</td></tr>
</table>

> **The longer** we live, **the more** our experience widens, **the less** prone are we to judge our neighbour's conduct.
>
> Charlotte Bronte, Villette

> ***More than*** and *less than* are compound modifiers.

adverb modifies "nothing"
> I am nothing **more than** a lions' provider: I do not feel at all sure that they will not growl and finally destroy me.
>
> Charles Darwin, The Life and Letters of Charles Darwin

An adverbial noun tells the time or place of an action, or explains how long, how far, how deep, how thick, or how much. It can modify a verb, adjective or adverb. An adverbial noun plus its modifiers is an adverbial noun phrase.

> It appears that sitting **one day** in the Cathedral of Pisa, Galileo's attention became concentrated on the swinging of a chandelier which hung from the ceiling.
>
> Robert S. Ball, Great Astronomers

An interrogative adverb asks a question.

> where, when, why, how

> **Why** do we have to go rushing on past all these lovely rooms?
>
> Roald Dahl, Charlie and the Chocolate Factory

> **The interrogative adverbs can also introduce noun clauses.**

noun clauses acting as objects of the infinitive
> I desired to know **how this thing came to Gollum**, and **how long he had possessed it.**
>
> J. R. R. Tolkien, The Fellowship of the Ring

An affirmation states what is true or what exists.
A negation states what is not true or does not exist.

> **Adverbs of Affirmation**

> yes, surely, definitely, certainly, absolutely, very

And yet I deserve everything, for I am **certainly very** stubborn and stupid!

C. Collodi, *The Adventures of Pinocchio*

Adverbs of Negation

no, not, never

I have **never** obeyed anyone and I have always done as I pleased.
C. Collodi, *The Adventures of Pinocchio*

Do not use two adverbs or adjectives of negation together.

Affirmative and negative adverbs can also act as interjections.

Yes, yes, yes! It is I! Look at me!

"Tell me, Lamp-Wick, dear friend, have you ever suffered from an earache?"
"**Never!** And you?"

C. Collodi, *The Adventures of Pinocchio*

PREPOSITIONS

A preposition shows the relationship of a noun or pronoun to another word in the sentence.

aboard, about, above, across, after, against, along, among, around, at
before, behind, below, beneath, beside, between, beyond, by
down, during
except
for, from
in, inside, into
like
near
of, off, on, over
past
since
through, throughout, to, toward, under, underneath
until, up, upon
with, within, without

A prepositional phrase begins with a preposition and ends with a noun or pronoun.
That noun or pronoun is the object of the preposition.

Prepositional phrases can act as nouns, adjectives, and adverbs.

But when Percival saw what he would be at, he catched up his javelin

adverb phrase modifying
"running" adverb phrase modifying
"threw"

and, running **to a little distance**, he turned and threw it **at Sir Boindegardus**

adjective phrase
modifying "point"

with so cunning an aim that the point **of the javelin** entered the

adjective phrase   adjective phrase
modifying "ocularium"   modifying "helmet"

ocularium of **the helmet of Sir Boindegardus** and pierced

adverb phrase   adverb phrase   adjective phrase
modifying "pierced"   modifying "out"   modifying "back"

through the eye and the brain and came out **of the back of the head.**

adjective phrase serving
as predicate adjective

Then those who were **of the Queen's court** told King Arthur what had

adjective phrase
modifying "displeasure"

befallen, and thereat the King felt great displeasure **toward Sir Kay.**

adjective phrase
modifying "thongs"

Thereupon he drew his misericordia, and he cut the thongs **of his harness**

adjective phrase   noun phrase serving as
modifying "pieces"   object of the preposition "from"

and he tore the pieces **of armor** from **off his body** and flung them away

adverb phrase   adverb phrase
modifying "flung"   modifying "flung"

very furiously, **upon the right hand** and **upon the left**.

So when King Arthur confirmed Sir Launcelot's permission, Sir Lionel

adverb phrase
modifying "early"

also made himself ready very joyfully, and early **of the morning**

adjective phrase   adjective phrase
modifying "morning"   modifying the noun "leave"

of the next day they two took their leave **of the court** and rode away
together; the day being very fair and gracious and all the air

adverb phrase   adjective phrase   noun phrase serving as   adjective phrase
modifying "full"   modifying "joy"   predicate nominative   modifying "flower"

full **of the joy of that season**--which was **in the flower of the spring-time**.

Howard Pyle, *The Story of the
Champions of the Round Table*

CONJUNCTIONS

A conjunction joins words or groups of words together.

A coordinating conjunction joins similar or equal words or groups of words together.

And, or, nor, for, so, but, yet

But Flopsy, Mopsy, **and** Cotton-tail had bread **and** milk **and** blackberries for supper.

Beatrix Potter, *The Tale of Peter Rabbit*

The independent clauses of a compound sentence must be joined by a comma and a coordinating conjunction, a semicolon, or a semicolon and a coordinating conjunction. They cannot be joined by a comma alone.

semicolon connects
independent clauses

Peter was most dreadfully frightened; he rushed all over the

comma and conjunction connects
two equal independent clauses

garden, **for** he had forgotten the way back to the gate.

Beatrix Potter, *The Tale of Peter Rabbit*

Compound subjects joined by *and* are plural in number and take plural verbs.

Flopsy, Mopsy, **and** Cotton-tail, who **were** good little bunnies, went down the lane to gather blackberries.

Beatrix Potter, *The Tale of Peter Rabbit*

When compound subjects are joined by *or,* the verb agrees with the number of the nearest subject.

Angry fairies, or an evil fairy, was present at the christening.

When compound subjects are connected by "not only . . . but/but also," "either . . . or," or "neither . . . nor," the verb agrees with the subject that is closest to the verb.

Neither the roof **nor** the **chimneys** of the castle **were** visible through the hedge of thorns.

A subordinating conjunction joins unequal words or groups of words together.

Then she took up Hansel with her rough hands, and shut him up in a

joins dependent clause to main clause

little cage with a lattice-door; and **although** <u>he screamed loudly</u> it was of

joins dependent clause to main clause
no use. She was envious, too, **because** <u>her step-daughter was beautiful</u>
<u>and lovely, and her own daughter was ugly and hateful.</u>

The Brothers Grimm

**When *than* is used in a comparison and introduces a clause with
understood elements, it is acting as a subordinating conjunction.**

clause has understood verb "was,"
"than" acts as subordinating conjunction
Three-Eyes, however, was not more fortunate **than** <u>her sister</u>, for the

"as soon as" is compound subordinating conjunction
golden apples flew back **as soon as** <u>she touched them</u>.

The Brothers Grimm

Correlative conjunctions work in pairs to join words or groups of words.

**Coordinating correlative conjunctions join equal words or groups of
words.**

both . . . and
not only . . . but/but also
either . . . or
neither . . . nor
although/though . . . yet/still
if . . . then

coordinating correlative conjunctions join compound predicate adjectives
Neither a borrower **nor** a lender be:

coordinating correlative conjunctions join compound direct objects
For loan oft loses **both** itself **and** friend;
And borrowing dulls the edge of husbandry.

coordinating correlative conjunctions join two independent clauses
Though this be madness, **yet** there is a method in't.

William Shakespeare, Hamlet

coordinating correlative conjunctions join two independent clauses
If it were done when 'tis done, **then** 'twere well
   It were done quickly.

William Shakespeare, Macbeth

**Subordinating correlative conjunctions join unequal words or groups
of words.**

although/though . . . yet/still
if . . . then

If a governor returns rich from his government, they say he has
subordinating correlative conjunctions join an adjective to an independent clause
fleec'd and robb'd the people; **if** poor, **then** they call him idle fool, an
ill husband.

> Miguel de Cervantes Saavedra, *Don Quixote*

preposition introducing adjective phrase   preposition introducing adjective phrase

Though troubled, they were not distressed; **though** perplexed,

preposition introducing
adjective phrase

not in despair; **though** persecuted, they were not forsaken;

subordinating correlative conjunctions join a past participle phrase acting as an adjective to an independent clause

though cast down, **yet** they were not destroyed.

> James Bandinel, "Suffering and Glory"

Quasi-coordinators link compound parts of a sentence or clause that are unequal. Quasi-coordinators include *rather than, sooner than, as well as, let alone,* and *not to mention.*

Quasi-coordinator links predicate adjective and adjective phrase

Those tiny bones are dangerous **as well as** troublesome to be eaten.

> Oliver Goldsmith, *A History of
> the Earth and Animated Nature*

Kepler had himself assigned no reason why the orbit of a planet should

Quasi-coordinator links simple predicate nominative to predicate nominative phrase modified by clause

be an ellipse **rather than** any other of the infinite number of closed curves which might be traced around the sun.

> Robert S. Ball, *Great Astronomers*

WORDS ACTING AS MULTIPLE PARTS OF SPEECH

Some words (such as *but, for, about, yet, any, before, above, after, otherwise, still*) can act as prepositions, subordinating conjunctions, adjectives, adverbs, nouns, or other parts of speech.

adverb

I could not reproach myself **any** less.

adjective

It would be an insult to the discernment of **any** man with half an eye to tell him so.

pronoun

I wonder whether **any** of the gentlemen remembered him.

> Charles Dickens, *Bleak House*

coordinating conjunction

The rider did not bridle him, **but** walked beside him, leading him by touch of hand, and together they passed slowly into the shade of the cottonwoods.

adjective

There never was any one **but** her in my life till now.

adverb

I never had **but** one idea. I never rested.

Zane Grey, *Riders of the Purple Sage*

SENTENCES

A sentence is a group of words that contains a subject and predicate. A sentence begins with a capital letter and ends with a punctuation mark. A sentence contains a complete thought.

(each sentence in this excerpt is a complete thought, although the last has no subject or predicate)

Can we measure intelligence without understanding it? Possibly so; physicists measured gravity and magnetism long before they understood them theoretically. Maybe psychologists can do the same with intelligence.

Or maybe not.

James W. Kalat, *Introduction to Psychology*

A statement gives information. A statement always ends with a period.

Statements are **declarative** sentences.

But at the time of which I write I had descended far past those familiar, manageable doldrums.

William Styron, *Darkness Visible: A Memoir of Madness*

An exclamation shows sudden or strong feeling. An exclamation always ends with an exclamation point.

Exclamations are **exclamatory** sentences.

A command gives an order or makes a request. A command ends with either a period or an exclamation point.

Commands are **imperative** sentences.

The subject of a command is understood to be you.

A question asks something. A question always ends with a question mark.

Questions are known as **interrogative** sentences.

Haven't we suffered long enough under the stereotypes and cruel jokes?
Adrienne Martini, *Hillbilly Gothic:*
A Memoir of Madness and Motherhood

**Interrogative adjectives modify nouns and answer the questions
"which one" and "how many."**
Interrogative pronouns take the place of nouns in questions.

who, whom, whose, what, which

**Use the helping verbs *do, does,* and *did* to form negatives, ask
questions, and provide emphasis.**

I asked her, **What does** the silver ball mean?

Did I talk faster than usual?

Kay Redfield Jamison,
An Unquiet Mind: A Memoir
of Moods and Madness

An interrogative adverb asks a question.

where, when, why, how

Where did he get the money? **Who** does he think he is?
Paul Gilbert, *Depression: The*
Evolution of Powerlessness

**A simple sentence contains one independent clause and no subordinate
clauses.**
**No matter what else is in a simple sentence, it will only have *one* subject-
predicate set in it.**

subject-predicate set
Rhetoric may be defined as the faculty of observing in any given case
the available means of persuasion.
Aristotle, *Rhetoric,* trans. W. Rhys Roberts

A complex sentence contains at least one subordinate clause.

main subject-predicate set   first subordinate clause
Persuasion is achieved by the speaker's personal character **when the**
second subordinate clause
speech is so spoken as to make us think him credible.
Aristotle, *Rhetoric,* trans. W. Rhys Roberts

A compound sentence is a sentence with two or more independent clauses.

The independent clauses of a compound sentence must be joined by a comma and a coordinating conjunction, a coordinating conjunction alone, a semicolon, or a semicolon and a coordinating conjunction. They cannot be joined by a comma alone.

Of the modes of persuasion some belong strictly to the art of rhetoric **and** some do not.

Aristotle, Rhetoric, trans. W. Rhys Roberts

A compound-complex sentence is made up of two or more independent clauses, at least one of which is a complex sentence.

first subject-predicate set
in first independent clause   first subordinate clause in first sentence
It is not true, **as some writers assume in their treatises on rhetoric, that**

second subordinate clause in first sentence
the personal goodness revealed by the speaker contributes nothing to

second subject-predicate set
in second independent clause
his power of persuasion; on the contrary, his **character may** almost **be**

subordinate clause in second sentence
with understood relative pronoun "that"
called the most effective means of persuasion **he possesses.**

Aristotle, Rhetoric, trans. W. Rhys Roberts

Conditional sentences express hypothetical situations.

A condition clause describes a circumstance that has not yet happened. A consequence clause describes the results that will take place if the condition clause happens.

First Conditional Sentences express circumstances that might actually happen.
The predicate of the condition clause is in a present tense.
The predicate of the consequence clause is an imperative or is in a present or future tense.

present tense (condition clause)   future tense (consequence clause)
If you **are** not perfectly **satisfied**, your wasted time **will be refunded.**

Norton Juster, The Phantom Tollbooth

Second Conditional Sentences express circumstances that are contrary to reality.
The predicate of the condition clause is in a past subjunctive tense.
The predicate of the consequence clause is in the simple or progressive present modal tense.

past subjunctive tense (condition clause)
If you **walked** as fast as possible and **looked** at nothing but your

simple present modal tense (consequence clause)
shoes, you **would arrive** at your destination more quickly.
Norton Juster, *The Phantom Tollbooth*

Third Conditional Sentences express past circumstances that never happened.
The predicate of the condition clause is in the perfect past tense.
The predicate of the consequence clause is in any modal tense.

modal tense (consequence clause)   perfect past tense (condition clause)
You **would have dropped him**, if a goblin **had** suddenly **grabbed** your legs from behind in the dark, **tripped** up your feet, and **kicked** you in the back!
J. R. R. Tolkien, *The Hobbit*

Formal conditional sentences drop "if" from the condition clause and reverse the order of the subject and helping verb.

condition clause   consequence clause
Were you not otherwise agreeable, I should be forced to remove your tongue with my saber.
Jane Austen and Seth Grahame-Smith,
Pride & Prejudice & Zombies

An equal sentence is made up of a series of independent grammatical elements.

Equal sentences can be segregating, freight-train, or balanced.

Segregating sentences express a single idea each, and occur in a series.

The barn was still dark. The sheep lay motionless. Even the goose was quiet.
E. B. White, *Charlotte's Web*

Freight-train sentences link independent clauses together to express a combined idea.

There was much game hanging outside the shops, and the snow powdered in the fur of the foxes and the wind blew their tails.
Ernest Hemingway, *In Another Country*

Balanced sentences are made up of two equal parts, separated by a pause.

Darkness is cheap, and Scrooge liked it.
Charles Dickens, *A Christmas Carol*

A subordinating sentence is made up of both independent and dependent elements.

In a loose sentence, subordinate constructions follow the main clause.

main clause   first subordinate clause—adverbial
The spotlight has often been focused on me because I was a late

adjective clause within
    adverbial clause   adverb phrase
bloomer who turned out to be a prodigy, and perhaps, more than that,

second subordinate
clause—adverbial
because I am a black woman excelling in a white world.

Misty Copeland, *Life in Motion: An Unlikely Ballerina*

In a periodic sentence, subordinate constructions precede the main clause.

infinitive phrases   main clause
To be, or not to be: that is the question.

William Shakespeare, *Hamlet*

A cumulative sentence puts multiple subordinate constructions before or after the main clause.

prepositional phrase   five adjectival clauses, all beginning with "that"
Beyond the obvious facts **that** he has at some time done manual labour,
that he takes snuff, **that** he is a Freemason, **that** he has been in China,
and **that** he has done a considerable amount of writing lately, I can
main clause
deduce nothing else.

A. Conan Doyle, "The Red-Headed League"

main clause
four noun clauses acting as direct objects, all introduced with
"how" and each containing additional subordinate elements
Lastly, she pictured to herself **how** this same little sister of hers
would, in the after-time, be herself a grown woman; and **how** she
would keep, through all her riper years, the simple and loving
heart of her childhood; and **how** she would gather about her other
little children, and make their eyes bright and eager with many a
strange tale, perhaps even with the dream of Wonderland of long
ago; and **how** she would feel with all their simple sorrows, and find
a pleasure in all their simple joys, remembering her own child-life,
and the happy summer days.

Lewis Carroll, *Alice's Adventures in Wonderland*

In a convoluted sentence, subordinate constructions divide the main clause.

adverbial prepositional phrase with multiple

subject of the   infinitives serving as objects of the compound

main clause   appositive phrase   preposition "in order"

We, the people of the United States, in order to form a more perfect union, establish justice, insure domestic tranquility, provide for the common defense, promote the general welfare, and secure the blessings

predicate of the main clause

of liberty to ourselves and our posterity, **do ordain and establish** this Constitution for the United States of America.

The Constitution of the United States

In a centered sentence, subordinate constructions come on both sides of the main clause.

participial phrase   adjectival subordinate clause

And having got rid of this young man who did not know how to

subject and compound predicate of main clause

behave, **she resumed** her duties as hostess and **continued** to listen

adjective phrase   adjective phrase introduced by relative adverb

and watch, ready to help at any point where the conversation might happen to flag.

Leo Tolstoy, *War and Peace*

PARTS OF SENTENCES

"Part of the sentence" is a term that explains how a word functions in a sentence.

SUBJECTS AND PREDICATES

The subject of the sentence is the main word or term that the sentence is about.

The simple subject of the sentence is *just* the main word or term that the sentence is about.

The complete subject of the sentence is the simple subject and all the words that belong to it.

The predicate of the sentence tells something about the subject.

The simple predicate of the sentence is the main verb along with any helping verbs.
The complete predicate of the sentence is the simple predicate and all the words that belong to it.

complete subject   complete predicate
    simple subject   simple predicate
An official <u>voice</u> | <u>was heard</u> exhorting the guests to leave a path for the procession.

complete subject   complete predicate
simple subject simple predicate
<u>She</u> | <u>was</u> one of those people who never feel they have said a thing till they have said it three times over.

complete predicate   complete subject
        simple predicate   simple subject
Folded within its walls <u>lay</u> | a trim grass <u>plot</u>, with flower-beds splashed at the angles, and surrounded by a wide stone plinth.

Dorothy Sayers, *Gaudy Night*

The subject and predicate of a sentence agree in person and number.

Compound subjects joined by *and* are plural in number and take plural verbs.

When the door had closed on the last of them and the chink of the
                compound subject   plural verb   plural verb
lanterns had died away, **Mole and Rat kicked** the fire up, **drew** their
            plural verb
chairs in, **brewed** themselves a last nightcap of mulled ale, and
plural verb
discussed the events of the long day.

Kenneth Grahame, *The Wind in the Willows*

Compound subjects joined by *and* take a singular verb when they name the same thing.

                                                                singular
        plural subject   plural verb   compound subject
If the **sheep have eaten** one part entirely bare, their **lord and master**
singular verb
    has only to drive them to another part.

Henry Lichtenstein, *Travels in Southern Africa*

When compound subjects are joined by *or*, the verb agrees with the number of the nearest subject.

                        plural verb
Steak or eggs **are** on offer for breakfast.

singular verb
Eggs or steak **is** on offer for breakfast.

When a fraction serves as a subject, it is singular when used to indicate a single thing. It is plural when used to indicate more than one thing.

singular verb
Three-fourths of the pie **was** missing.

plural verb
Three-fourths of the socks **were** missing.

Expressions of money, time, and quantity (weight, units, and distance) are singular when used as a whole, but plural when used of numerous single units.

plural verb
Fifteen hundred dollars **were handed** out to eleven hundred lottery winners.

singular verb
Fifteen hundred dollars **was listed** as the lowest bid.

Collective nouns are usually singular. Collective nouns can be plural if the members of the group are acting as independent individuals.

singular verb
The herd of cattle **was grazing** quietly.

plural verb
The herd of cattle **were scattered** throughout the plains.

Many nouns can be plural in form but singular in use: measles, mumps, rickets, politics, mathematics, economics, news.

singular verb
Mathematics **is** my favorite subject.

Many nouns are plural in form and use but singular in meaning: pants, scissors, pliers, glasses.

plural verb, but singular in meaning
Pants **are** too hot in the summertime.

Singular literary works, works of art, newspapers, countries, and organizations can be plural in form but are still singular in use.

singular verb
Little Women **was written** by Louisa May Alcott.

singular verb
The United States **is** south of Canada.

In sentences beginning with *There is* or *There are*, the subject is found after the verb.

There <u>is</u> a <u>skunk</u> in the brush.

There <u>are</u> three <u>skunks</u> in the brush.

Each **and** ***every*** **always indicate a singular subject.**

singular verb

In Masai villages, **each** of the women **cares** for her own cattle.

plural verb

In Masai villages, women **care** for their own cattle.

Compound nouns that are plural in form but singular in meaning take a singular verb.

singular verb

Fish and chips is my favorite British dish.

Nouns with Latin and Greek origins take the singular verb when singular in form and the plural verb when plural in form.

Singular	Plural
medium	media
datum	data
criterion	criteria
phenomenon	phenomena
focus	foci
appendix	appendices

singular verb

This **phenomenon is** unusual.

plural verb

These **phenomena are** unusual.

OBJECTS

A direct object receives the action of the verb.

subject   predicate   direct object

<u>Aunt Polly</u> <u>placed</u> small **trust** in such evidence.

Mark Twain, *The Adventures of Tom Sawyer*

An object complement follows the direct object and renames or describes it.

subject predicate   direct object object complement   object complement

<u>She</u> <u>found</u> the entire **fence whitewashed,** and not only **whitewashed**

object complement   object complement

but elaborately **coated** and **recoated**, and even a streak added to the ground.

Mark Twain, *The Adventures of Tom Sawyer*

An indirect object is the noun or pronoun for whom or to whom an action is done.
An indirect object comes between the action verb and the direct object.

action indirect direct
verb   object   object

A servant hurried up and offered **Loki** wine.

Kevin Crossley-Holland, The Norse Myths

A prepositional phrase begins with a preposition and ends with a noun or pronoun.
That noun or pronoun is the object of the preposition.

object of the preposition   object of the preposition

<u>Beneath **Loki**</u> the world seemed very small: he looked down <u>at the **trees**</u> and

object of the preposition

the mountains, tiny as children's playthings, and the problems <u>of the **gods**</u> seemed a small thing also.

Neil Gaiman, Norse Mythology

PHRASES

A phrase is a group of words serving a single grammatical function.

A prepositional phrase begins with a preposition and ends with a noun or pronoun.
That noun or pronoun is the object of the preposition.

A prepositional phrase that describes a noun or pronoun is called an adjective phrase.

A prepositional phrase that describes a verb, adjective, or adverb is called an adverb phrase.

A prepositional phrase can act as an adjective, adverb, subject, predicate adjective, predicate nominative, or object of the preposition

predicate adjective   adjective
modifying "father and son"   modifying "ideas"

Father and son were **at chess,** the former, who possessed ideas **about the**

adverb modifying "putting" and
answering the question "where"

game involving radical changes, putting his king **into such sharp and**

adjective modifying "comment"

unnecessary perils that it even provoked comment **from the white-**

adverb modifying "knitting" and
answering the question "where"

haired old lady knitting placidly **by the fire.**

W. W. Jacobs, "The Monkey's Paw"

Her mind, and especially her memory, was preternaturally active, and

adjective modifying "street"

kept bringing up other scenes than this roughly hewn street **of a little**

adjective   adjective
modifying "town"   modifying "edge"

town, on the edge **of the western wilderness**: other faces than were
lowering

adverb modifying   adverb modifying
"were lowering"   "were lowering"   adjective modifying "brims"

upon her **from** beneath the brims **of those steeple-crowned hats**.

object of the
preposition "from"   Nathaniel Hawthorne, *The Scarlet Letter*

A verb phrase is the main verb plus any helping verbs.

No more **be griev'd** at that which thou **hast done**:
Roses have thorns, and silver fountains mud.
                                        William Shakespeare, "Sonnet XXXV"

A phrase that modifies a noun or prounoun is called an adjective phrase.
   Adjective phrases usually come directly after the words they modify.
      **A misplaced modifier is an adjective, adjective phrase, adverb, or
      adverb phrase in the wrong place.**
      **A squinting modifier can belong either to the sentence element
      preceding or the element following.**
      A dangling modifier has no noun or verb to modify.

   See misplaced, squinting, and dangling modifiers on p. 37.

**A phrase that modifies a verb, adjective, or adverb is called an adverb
phrase.**
   Adverb phrases can be anywhere in a sentence.

                    adverb phrase   adjective phrase
                    modifying "preserved"   modifying "preparation"

They preserved peace **by a constant preparation** **for war**; and while justice

                    adverb phrase   adjective phrase
                    modifying "announced" modifying "nations"

regulated their conduct, they announced **to the nations** **on their confines**,

                    adverb phrase   adverb phrase
                    modifying "disposed"   modifying "disposed"

that they were as little disposed **to endure**, as **to offer an injury**.
                                        Edward Gibbon, *The History of the Decline
                                        and Fall of the Roman Empire,* Vol. 1

adverb phrase telling "when"
   adjective phrase
within adverb phrase,   (predicate) adjective phrase
   modifying "midst"   modifying "we"

In the midst **of life**, we are **in death**.
                                        The Book of Common Prayer

A phrase that takes the place of a noun and acts as a subject, object, predicate nominative, appositive, or absolute construction is a noun phrase.

participle phrase acting as subject
> **Running away** is contrary to the practice of the place.
> > Hastings H. Hart, *Plans and Illustrations*
> > *of Prisons and Reformatories*

infinitive phrase acting as direct object
> He loved **to have the cloth laid**, because it had been the fashion of his
prepostional phrase acting as appositive
> youth; but his conviction **of suppers being very unwholesome** made him rather sorry to see any thing put on it; and while his hospitality would have welcomed his visitors to every thing, his care for their health made him grieve that they would eat.
> > Jane Austen, *Emma*

infinitives acting as absolute constructions
> **To die**,—**to sleep**;—
> **To sleep**! perchance **to dream**:—ay, there's the rub.
> > William Shakespeare, *Hamlet*

CLAUSES

A clause is a group of words that contains a subject and a predicate.

> A surprising development was the American colony of the Philippines,
> subject   predicate
> <u>which</u> <u>was</u> not simply an unforeseen consequence of the Spanish-American War of 1898.
> > Arthur Cotterell, *A History of Southeast Asia*

An independent clause can stand by itself as a sentence.

> God never made a human being either for destruction or degradation.
> > William Lloyd Garrison, "No Compromise with Slavery"

A dependent clause is a fragment that cannot stand by itself as a sentence.

> **Dependent clauses begin with subordinating words.**
> **Dependent clauses are also known as subordinate clauses.**

dependent clause
subordinating words
> His hoof-beats ring upon our slopes at sunrise **<u>as though</u> our fields were of silver.**
> > Lord Dunsany, *Fifty-One Tales*

Dependent clauses can act as adjective clauses, adverb clauses, or noun clauses.

An adjective clause is a dependent clause that acts as an adjective in a sentence, modifying a noun or pronoun in the independent clause.

Relative pronouns introduce adjective clauses and refer back to an antecedent in the independent clause.

who, whom, whose, which, that

relative pronoun refers back to
"those" and introduces adjective clause

Those **who** seek to obtain it from a banana blossom at midnight

relative pronoun refers back to
"demons" and introduces adjective clause

must fight off the demons **that** guard it.

Alex G. Paman, *Filipino Ghost Stories.*

Adjective clauses can be introduced by prepositions.

Adjective clauses should usually go immediately before or after the noun or pronoun they modify.

Uncas found himself walking a treacherous path between the

preposition introduces adjective clause
modifying and immediately following "natives"

English and the natives **over** whom he exerted his influence.

Michael L. Oberg, *Native America: A History*

A restrictive modifying clause defines the word that it modifies. Removing the clause changes the essential meaning of the sentence.

A nonrestrictive modifying clause describes the word that it modifies. Removing the clause doesn't change the essential meaning of the sentence.

Only nonrestrictive clauses should be set off by commas.

restrictive adjective clause

The idea **that a stranger may expire on your doorstep from hunger** cannot be tolerated.

nonrestrictive adjective clause

The feast of Tara was held, **at which all were gathered together**.

James Stephens, *Irish Fairy Tales*

The interrogative words who, whom, whose, what, and which can also serve as relative pronouns in adjective clauses or introductory words in noun clauses.

adjective clause modifying "government"
relative pronoun with "government" as antecedent

Show me the government **which** <u>can be maintained only by</u> <u>destroying the rights of a portion of the people</u>; and you will indicate the duty of openly revolting against it.

noun clause acting as direct object

I care not **what** <u>caste, creed or colour, Slavery may assume</u>.

William Lloyd Garrison,
"No Compromise with Slavery"

Relative adverbs introduce adjective clauses and refer back to a place, time, or reason in the independent clause.

where, when, why

relative adverb with   adjective clause
"winter" as antecedent   modifying "winter"

He arrived here in the deep winter **when** <u>the Founders were under</u> <u>attack from many foxes, vermin, and a great wildcat.</u>

Brian Jacques, *Redwall*

Adverb clauses modify verbs, adjectives, and other adverbs in the independent clause. They answer the questions where, when, how, how often, and to what extent.

adverb clause answers
the question "when"

We do not enlarge but disfigure the sciences **when we lose sight of their respective limits and allow them to run into one another.**

Immanuel Kant, *The Critique of Pure Reason*

Adverb clauses can be introduced by adverbs.

adverb clause modifies "grinned"
adverb

His teeth were long and sharp and grinned horribly, **while** <u>his lower</u> <u>lip hung down upon his chest</u>, and he had ears like elephant's ears.

Andrew Lang, *The Arabian*
Nights Entertainments

Subordinating conjunctions and subordinating correlative conjunctions often join an adverb clause to an independent clause.

after
although
as (as soon as)
because
before
if

in order that
lest
since
though
till
unless
until
although/though . . . yet/still
if . . . then

adverb clause modifying "believe"
subordinating conjunction

I cannot believe it **<u>unless</u> <u>I see you do the thing</u>**.

adverb clause modifying "earlier"
subordinating conjunction

That morning the princess rose earlier **<u>than</u> <u>she had done</u>**

adverb clause modifying "had done"
subordinating conjunction

<u>since</u> <u>she had been carried away by the magician</u>.
Andrew Lang, *The Arabian Nights Entertainments*

A noun clause takes the place of a noun. Noun clauses can be introduced by relative pronouns, relative adverbs, interrogative adverbs, or subordinating conjunctions.

Although this exposition is of great importance, it does not belong essentially to the main purpose of the work, because the grand question is

noun clause introduced by relative pronoun/interrogative adverb combination, serves as half of compound predicate nominative renaming "question"

what and how much can reason and understanding, apart from

noun clause introduced by interrogative adverb,
serving as second half of compound predicate nominative

experience, cognize, and not, **how is the faculty of thought itself possible?**
Immanuel Kant, *The Critique of Pure Reason*

A dependent clause can act as an appositive if it renames the noun that it follows.

appositive noun clause renames "decree"

There was a decree **that no ship should sail from any post with**

appositive phrase
renames "Jason"

more than five hands on board, but Jason alone, **the master of the great ship Argo**, should cruise about, and keep the sea free of pirates.

Plutarch, *Plutarch's Lives*, Vol. 1, trans.
Aubrey Stewart and George Long

The interrogative adverbs can also introduce noun clauses.

where, when, why, how

Akademus, who had by some means discovered that she was

noun clause acting
as direct object

concealed at Aphidnae, now told them **where** <u>she was</u>.

Plutarch, *Plutarch's Lives*, Vol. 1, trans.
Aubrey Stewart and George Long

A noun clause can have an understood introductory word.

four noun clauses, each acting as direct object and introduced with understood "that"

I know **he meant no harm**; I never said **he did**; I know **he is not a bad boy**, but you see **I am sore myself**.

Anna Sewall, *Black Beauty*

A condition clause describes a circumstance that has not yet happened. A consequence clause describes the results that will take place if the condition clause happens.

See Conditional Sentences, p. 46.

First Conditional Sentences express circumstances that might actually happen.
The predicate of the condition clause is in a present tense.
The predicate of the consequence clause is an imperative or is in a present or future tense.

Second Conditional Sentences express circumstances that are contrary to reality.
The predicate of the condition clause is in a past tense.
The predicate of the consequence clause is in the simple present modal tense.

Third Conditional Sentences express past circumstances that never happened.
The predicate of the condition clause is in the perfect past tense.
The predicate of the consequence clause is in the perfect present modal or simple present modal tense.

PARENTHETICAL ELEMENTS

Parenthetical expressions often interrupt or are irrelevant to the rest of the sentence.

> The tradesmen came while we were yet speaking; and we moved in a body to old Dr. Denman's surgical theatre, from which (as you are doubtless aware) Jekyll's private cabinet is most conveniently entered.
> Robert Louis Stevenson, *Dr. Jekyll and Mr. Hyde*

> Trolls simply detest the sight of dwarves (uncooked).
> J. R. R. Tolkien, *The Hobbit*

Parentheses ( ) can enclose words that are not essential to the sentence. Parentheses minimize a parenthetical element.

> Alice ventured to taste it, and finding it very nice (it had, in fact, a sort of mixed flavour of cherry tart, custard, pineapple, roast turkey, toffee, and hot buttered toast) she very soon finished it off.
> Lewis Carroll, *Alice's Adventures in Wonderland*

Dashes — — can enclose words that are not essential to the sentence.
Dashes emphasize a parenthetical element.
Dashes can also be used singly to separate parts of a sentence.

> Humpty Dumpty was sitting with his legs crossed, like a Turk, on the top of a high wall—such a narrow one that Alice quite wondered how he could keep his balance—and, as his eyes were steadily fixed in the opposite direction, and he didn't take the least notice of her, she thought he must be a stuffed figure after all.

> But the beard seemed to melt away as she touched it, and she found herself sitting quietly under a tree—while the Gnat (for that was the insect she had been talking to) was balancing itself on a twig just over her head, and fanning her with its wings.
> Lewis Carroll, *Through the Looking-Glass*

Dashes and parentheses always turn a clause or phrase into a parenthetical element, even if there is a grammatical relationship between the clause or phrase and the rest of the sentence.

adverb phrase, turned
into parenthetical element

> "Here are the Red King and the Red Queen," Alice said (in a whisper, for fear of frightening them), "and there are the White King and the White Queen sitting on the edge of the shovel."
> Lewis Carroll, *Through the Looking-Glass*

Punctuation goes inside the parentheses or dashes if it applies to the parenthetical material; all other punctuation goes outside the parentheses or dashes.

This, then, is the last time, short of a miracle, that Henry Jekyll can think his own thoughts or see his own face (now how sadly altered!) in the glass.

Never (she used to say, with streaming tears, when she narrated that experience), never had she felt more at peace with all men or thought more kindly of the world.

> Robert Louis Stevenson, *Dr. Jekyll and Mr. Hyde*

Parenthetical material only begins with a capital letter if it is a complete sentence with ending punctuation.

"Here's the place," she said at last, "and here we have yesterday's luncheon duly entered. One glass lemonade (Why can't you drink water, like me?) three sandwiches (They never put in half mustard enough. I told the young woman so, to her face; and she tossed her head—like her impudence!) and seven biscuits."

> Lewis Carroll, *A Tangled Tale*

Commas make a parenthetical element a part of the sentence.

If a clause or phrase is set off by commas, but doesn't have a clear grammatical relationship to the rest of the sentence, it is parenthetical.

We met the Colonel and his wife, who, **we thought**, were very agreeable people.

> Jack London, *White Fang*

INTERJECTIONS

Interjections express sudden feeling or emotion. They are set off with commas or stand alone with a closing punctuation mark.

Oh, we've all read a lot about pale-faced phantoms in the dark; but this was more dreadful than anything of that kind could ever be.

> G. K. Chesterton, *The Wisdom of Father Brown*

"**Oh!** if you are going to be paradoxical," said Rupert contemptuously, "be a bit funnier than that."

> G. K. Chesterton, *The Club of Queer Trades*

DIRECT ADDRESS

Nouns of direct address name a person or thing who is being spoken to.
They are set off with commas. They are capitalized only if they are proper
names or titles.

Friends, Romans, countrymen, lend me your ears!
William Shakespeare, *Julius Caesar*

APPOSITIVES

An appositive is a noun or noun phrase that usually follows another noun
and renames or explains it. Appositives are usually set off by commas.

nouns rename "Kozel"
There is the house of Kozel, **the cabinet-maker, a German**, well-to-do.
Fyodor Dostoevsky, *Crime and Punishment,*
trans. Constance Garnett

He was a short, square man with a dark, square face clean-shaven,
noun phrase renames "man"
a medical practitioner going by the name of Bull.
G. K. Chesterton, *The Man Who Was Thursday*

A dependent clause can act as an appositive if it renames the noun that it
follows.

clause renames "mystery"
Mr. Vernon demanded of his daughter the solution of the mystery, **how she
came to be alone in the carriage**.
Marguerite Blessington, "The Repealers"

clause renames "theory"
Mach's discovery led to his first theory, **that the whole human body
contributed to the sensation of motion**.
John T. Blackmore, *Ernst Mach:
His Work, Life, and Influence*

ABSOLUTE CONSTRUCTIONS

An absolute construction has a strong semantic relationship but no
grammatical connection to the rest of the sentence.

prepositional phrase in absolute construction
As to the door being locked, it is a very ordinary lock.
Agatha Christie, *The Mysterious Affair at Styles*

noun phrase in absolute construction
He went down, **rider and steed**, before his lance.
Henry Bulwer-Lytton, *Rienzi: The Last of the Tribunes*

noun modified by adjective clause and participle
phrase in absolute construction
He was buried in Westminster Abbey, **the stone that bears his inscription resting at the feet of Addison**.
Anonymous obituary of historian Thomas Macaulay

DIALOGUE AND QUOTATIONS

Use dialogue in fiction and to bring other voices into memoir, profiles, and reporting.

Dialogue is set off by quotation marks.

"How sober you look, child!" said Marie.
Harriet Beecher Stowe, *Uncle Tom's Cabin*

A quote within a quote is surrounded by single quotation marks.

"Yes—'after life's fitful fever they sleep well,'" I muttered. "Where are you going now, Mrs. Fairfax?"
Charlotte Bronte, *Jane Eyre*

A dialogue tag identifies the person making the speech.

When **she said**, "I pity your wife," "So do I pity you," **answered he**, "that without being a prisoner you stay with Alexander."
Plutarch, *Plutarch's Lives,* Vol. 2, trans.
Aubrey Stewart and George Long

When a dialogue tag comes after a speech, place a comma, exclamation point, or question mark inside the closing quotation marks.

"Let us climb up the rockery, and sit on the garden wall," said Moppet.

"It's a very fine morning!" said Mr. Drake Puddle-Duck.
Beatrix Potter, *The Tale of Tom Kitten*

When a dialogue tag comes before a speech, place a comma after the tag. Put the dialogue's final punctuation mark inside the closing quotation marks.

The young Mole said, "It is a pebble."

Aesop's Fables

Usually, a new paragraph begins with each new speaker.

When a dialogue tag comes in the middle of a speech, follow it with a comma if the following dialogue is an incomplete sentence. Follow it with a period if the following dialogue is a complete sentence.

Speeches do not need to be attached to a dialogue tag as long as the text clearly indicates the speaker.

"Not until he says what he means by lots and none at all," said Bert. "I don't want to have me throat cut in me sleep! Hold his toes in the fire, till he talks!"

"I won't have it," said William. "I caught him anyway."

"You're a fat fool, William," said Bert, "as I've said afore this evening."

"And you're a lout!"

"And I won't take that from you, Bill Huggins," says Bert, and puts his fist in William's eye.

J. R. R. Tolkien, *The Hobbit*

Use direct quotations to provide examples, cite authorities, and emphasize your own points.
Direct quotations are set off by quotation marks.

And, as the king list tells us, during his reign he "entered the seas and ascended the mountains."

Susan Wise Bauer, *The History of the Ancient World*

A quote within a quote is surrounded by single quotation marks.

Fear of spiders might come in part from children's stories, which often portray spiders as hostile predators. In *Glinda of Oz,* L. Frank Baum writes about a Spider King and his army of "great purple spiders, which . . . said, 'The web is finished, O King, and the strangers are our prisoners.'"

When an attribution tag comes after a direct quote, place a comma, exclamation point, or question mark inside the closing quotation marks.

"These are no lies!" one victory inscription ends up.
Susan Wise Bauer, The History
of the Ancient World

When an attribution tag comes before a direct quote, place a comma after the tag. Put the dialogue's final punctuation mark inside the closing quotation marks.

In the Roman countryside, Livy writes, "there was neither assured peace nor open war."
Susan Wise Bauer, The History
of the Ancient World

When an attribution tag comes in the middle of a direct quotation, follow it with a comma if the remaining quote is an incomplete sentence. Follow it with a period if the remaining quote is a complete sentence.

"Enlil," the fragment announces, "decided to remove the prosperity of the palace."

"For a long time he failed to observe that his bowels were ulcerated, till at length the corrupted flesh broke out into lice," Plutarch writes. "Many were employed day and night in destroying them, but the work so multiplied under their hands, that not only his clothes, baths, basins, but his very meat was polluted with that flux and contagion, they came swarming out in such numbers."
Susan Wise Bauer, The History
of the Ancient World

Every direct quote must have an attribution tag.

An attribution tag may be indirect.

In the wild songs of the slaves he read, beneath their senseless jargon or their fulsome praise of "old master," the often unconscious note of grief and despair.
Charles Chesnutt, Frederick Douglass

A second or third quote from the same source does not need another attribution tag, as long as context makes the source of the quote clear.

Direct quotes can be words, phrases, clauses, or sentences, as long as they are set off by quotation marks and form part of a grammatically correct original sentence.

If a direct quotation is longer than three lines, indent the entire quote one inch from the margin in a separate block of text and omit quotation marks.

When using a word processor, leave an additional line space before and after a block quote.

Block quotes should be introduced by a colon (if preceded by a complete sentence) or a comma (if preceded by a partial sentence).

If you change or make additions to a direct quotation, use brackets.

Ellipses show where something has been cut out of a direct quote.

The Roman historian Appian, who wrote his *Civil Wars* some two hundred years later, describes the general procedure for territory seized on the Italian peninsula:

> As the Romans conquered the Italian tribes, one after another, in war, they seized part of the lands. . . . Since they had not time to [sell or rent] the part which lay waste by the war, and this was usually the greater portion, they issued a proclamation that for the time being any who cared to work it could do so for a share of the annual produce . . . The wealthy, getting hold of most of the unassigned lands . . . and adding, part by purchase and part by violence, the little farms of their poor neighbors to their possessions, came to work great districts instead of one estate.

To work these large tracts, landowners needed plenty of labor.
Susan Wise Bauer, *The History
of the Ancient World*

A direct quote can be introduced by a colon.

The official murders soon progressed beyond the political and encompassed the personal as well: "More were killed for their property," Plutarch writes, "and even the executioners tended to say that this man was killed by his large house, this one by his garden, that one by his warm springs."
Susan Wise Bauer, *The History of the Ancient World*

To quote three or fewer lines of poetry, indicate line breaks by using a slanted line and retain all original punctuation and capitalization.

Likewise, Paul Laurence Dunbar's 1895 poem "We Wear the Mask" anticipates the "two-ness" of African-American existence expressed most poignantly and poetically by Du Bois nearly a decade later. Dunbar most famously writes: "We wear the mask that grins and lies,/It hides our cheeks and shades our eyes,—/This debt we pay to human guile."
Rebecca Rutledge Fisher, *Habitations of the Veil*

Four or more lines of poetry should be treated as a block quote.

In his poem, "We Wear the Mask," Dunbar speaks of a double-consciousness that had been forced on African Americans:

> We wear the mask that grins and lies,
> It hides our cheeks and shades our eyes,—
> This debt we pay to human guile;
> With torn and bleeding hearts we smile,
> And mouth with myriad subtleties.

Dunbar's biographer, Benjamin Brawley, wrote that Dunbar's poetry "soared above race and touched the heart universal."

Joseph Nazel, *Langston Hughes: Poet*

Any poetic citation longer than one line may be treated as a block quote.

Direct quotes should be properly documented.
See "Documentation," pages 76-77.

CAPITALIZATION: A SUMMARY OF ALL RULES

Capitalizing Nouns:

1. **Capitalize the proper names of persons, places, things, and animals.**
2. **Capitalize the names of holidays.**
3. **Capitalize the names of deities.**
4. **Capitalize the days of the week and the months of the year, but not the seasons.**
5. **Capitalize the first, last, and other important words in titles of books, magazines, newspapers, stories, poems, and songs.**
6. **Capitalize and italicize the names of ships, trains, and planes.**

A proper adjective is formed from a proper name. Proper adjectives are capitalized.

Words that are not usually capitalized remain lower-case even when they are attached to a proper adjective.

A sentence begins with a capital letter and ends with a punctuation mark.

Parenthetical material only begins with a capital letter if it is a complete sentence with ending punctuation.

Nouns of direct address name a person or thing who is being spoken to. They are set off with commas. They are capitalized only if they are proper names or titles.

The titles mister, madame, and miss are capitalized and abbreviated Mr., Mrs., and Miss when placed in front of a proper name.

Capitalize the personal pronoun I.

Capitalize the interjection O. It is usually preceded by, but not followed by, a comma.

> For a few weeks it was all well enough, but afterwards, O the weary length of the nights!
>
> Kenneth Grahame, *The Wind in the Willows*

After an interjection followed by an exclamation point, the next word may be lower case.

> Oh! let me see it once again before I die!
>
> Charles Dickens, *The Life and Adventures of Nicholas Nickleby*

Abbreviations are typically capitalized when each letter stands for something.

> Why did NASA cancel the lunar exploration program?

Capitalize the first word in every line of traditional poetry.

> When people call this beast to mind,
> They marvel more and more
> At such a little tail behind,
> So large a trunk before.
>
> Hilaire Belloc, "The Elephant"

Capitalize the date, address, greeting, closing, and signature of a letter.

Your Street Address
Your City, State, and ZIP Code

September 14, 2016

Well-Trained Mind Press
18021 The Glebe Lane
Charles City, Virginia 23030

Dear Editors:

Thank you for *Grammar for the Well-Trained Mind.* It is the most exciting grammar book I have ever read. I only wish I could spend more time doing grammar.

Please publish more grammar books immediately.

Sincerely,

Your Greatest Fan

Your Street Address
Your City, State, and ZIP Code

September 14, 2016

Well-Trained Mind Press
18021 The Glebe Lane
Charles City, Virginia 23030

Dear Editors:

Thank you for *Grammar for the Well-Trained Mind.* It is the most exciting grammar book I have ever read. I only wish I could spend more time doing grammar.

Please publish more grammar books immediately.

Sincerely,

Your Greatest Fan

PUNCTUATION: A SUMMARY OF ALL RULES

APOSTROPHES

An apostrophe is a punctuation mark that shows possession. It turns a noun into an adjective that tells whose.

> Form the possessive of a singular noun by adding an apostrophe and the letter *s*.
> Form the possessive of a plural noun ending in *-s* by adding an apostrophe only.
> Form the possessive of a plural noun that does not end in *-s* as if it were a singular noun.

A contraction is a combination of two words with some of the letters dropped out. An apostrophe replaces the missing letters.

CONTRACTION	MEANING	NOT THE SAME AS
he's	he is	his
she's	she is	her
it's	it is	its
you're	you are	your
they're	they are	their

BRACKETS

If you change or make additions to a direct quotation, use brackets.

COMMAS

Commas make a parenthetical element a part of the sentence.

The independent clauses of a compound sentence must be joined by a comma and a coordinating conjunction, a semicolon, or a semicolon and a coordinating conjunction. They cannot be joined by a comma alone.

When a dialogue tag comes after a speech, place a comma, exclamation point, or question mark inside the closing quotation marks.

When a dialogue tag comes before a speech, place a comma after the tag.

When a dialogue tag comes in the middle of a speech, follow it with a comma if the following dialogue is an incomplete sentence. Follow it with a period if the following dialogue is a complete sentence.

When an attribution tag comes after a direct quote, place a comma, exclamation point, or question mark inside the closing quotation marks.

When an attribution tag comes before a direct quote, place a comma after the tag. Put the dialogue's final punctuation mark inside the closing quotation marks.

When an attribution tag comes in the middle of a direct quotation, follow it with a comma if the remaining quote is an incomplete sentence. Follow it with a period if the remaining quote is a complete sentence.

Interjections express sudden feeling or emotion. They are set off with commas or stand alone with a closing punctuation mark.

Nouns of direct address name a person or thing who is being spoken to. They are set off with commas. They are capitalized only if they are proper names or titles.

Commas set off parenthetical expressions that are closely related to the sentence.

Short parenthetical expressions such as the following are usually set off by commas: *in short, in fact, in reality, as it were, as it happens, no doubt, in a word, to be sure, to be brief, after all, you know, of course.*

Commas may surround or follow interjections.

> Capitalize the interjection *O*. It is usually preceded by, but not followed by, a comma.

Commas separate three or more items in a series.

Commas separate two or more adjectives that come before a noun (as long as the adjectives can exchange position).

> All the rest of her time was spent in some low-ceiled, oaken chamber of the second storey.
>
> Charlotte Bronte, *Jane Eyre*

A comma follows the last adjective in a series of three or more (the "Oxford comma").

> INCORRECT: She invited her parents, Oprah Winfrey and Bono.
> CORRECT: She invited her parents, Oprah Winfrey, and Bono.

Commas set off terms of direct address.

Commas set off nonrestrictive adjective clauses.

Commas set off most appositives (unless the appositive is only one word and very closely related to the word it renames).

Commas may surround or follow introductory adverbs of affirmation and negation.

Commas may set off introductory adverb and adjective phrases.

In dates, commas separate the day of the week from the day of the month and the day of the month from the year.

In addresses, commas separate the city from the state.

Commas follow the greeting and closing of a friendly letter, and the closing of a formal letter.

Commas divide large numbers into sets of thousands.

A comma may divide a partial sentence from the block quote it introduces.

Commas may be used at any time to prevent misunderstanding and simplify reading.

If items in a series contain commas within the items, semicolons may separate two or more items in a series.

COLONS

Block quotes should be introduced by a colon (if preceded by a complete sentence) or a comma (if preceded by a partial sentence).

Use a colon after the salutation of a business letter.

Use a colon to separate the hour from minutes in a time.

Use a colon to separate the chapter from verse in a Biblical reference.

If semicolons separate items in a series, a colon may set off the series.

> Like the Great Pyramid, the Sphinx has attracted its share of nutty theories: it dates from 10,000 BC and was built by a disappeared advanced civilization; it was built by Atlanteans (or aliens); it represents a zodiacal sign, or a center of global energy.
> Susan Wise Bauer, *The History of the Ancient World*

A colon may introduce or follow a list.

> Plague, drought, and war: these were enough to upset the balance of a civilization that had been built in rocky dry places, close to the edge of survival.
> Susan Wise Bauer, *The History of the Ancient World*

A colon may introduce an item that follows a complete sentence, when that item is closely related to the sentence.

But the historian's task is different: to look for particular human lives that give flesh and spirit to abstract assertions about human behavior.
Susan Wise Bauer, *The History of the Ancient World*

DASHES

Dashes — — can enclose words that are not essential to the sentence.
Dashes emphasize a parenthetical element.

Dashes can also be used singly to separate parts of a sentence.

ELLIPSES

Ellipses show where something has been cut out of a sentence.

EXCLAMATION POINTS

An exclamation shows sudden or strong feeling. An exclamation always ends with an exclamation point.

A command gives an order or makes a request. A command ends with either a period or an exclamation point.

When a dialogue tag comes after a speech, place a comma, exclamation point, or question mark inside the closing quotation marks.

When an attribution tag comes after a direct quote, place a comma, exclamation point, or question mark inside the closing quotation marks.

After an interjection followed by an exclamation point, the next word may be lower case.

HYPHENS

Hyphens connect compound adjectives in the attributive position.
Compound adjectives in the predicative position are not usually hyphenated.

Hyphens connect some compound nouns.

> self-confidence
> wallpaper
> air conditioning

Hyphens connect compound adjectives in the attributive position.

> self-confident woman
> the woman was self confident

Hyphens connect spelled-out numbers between twenty-one and ninety-nine.

> seventy-one balloons
> he turned seventy-one on Friday

Hyphens divide words between syllables at the end of lines in justified text.

ITALICS

Capitalize and italicize the names of ships, trains, and planes.

Italicize the titles of lengthy or major works such as books, newspapers, magazines, major works of art, and long musical compositions.

Italicize letters, numbers, and words if they are the subject of discussion. In plural versions, do not italicize the s.

> Most Americans hate the word *moist.*

Italicize foreign words not adopted into English.

> What we call "rapid-eye-movement sleep" the French call *sommeil paradoxal* (paradoxical sleep) because the body is still but the mind is extremely active.
> Pamela Druckerman, *Bringing Up Bébé*

PARENTHESES

Parentheses ( ) can enclose words that are not essential to the sentence. Parenthetical expressions often interrupt or are irrelevant to the rest of the sentence. Parentheses minimize a parenthetical element.

Punctuation goes inside the parentheses if it applies to the parenthetical material; all other punctuation goes outside the parentheses.

Parenthetical material only begins with a capital letter if it is a complete sentence with ending punctuation.

Parenthetical expressions can also be set off by commas.

Short parenthetical expressions such as the following are usually set off by commas: in short, in fact, in reality, as it were, as it happens, no doubt, in a word, to be sure, to be brief, after all, you know, of course.

PERIODS

A statement gives information. A statement always ends with a period.

A command gives an order or makes a request. A command ends with either a period or an exclamation point.

When a dialogue tag comes in the middle of a speech, follow it with a period if the following dialogue is a complete sentence.

When an attribution tag comes in the middle of a direct quotation, follow it with a comma if the remaining quote is an incomplete sentence. Follow it with a period if the remaining quote is a complete sentence.

QUESTION MARKS

A question asks something. A question always ends with a question mark.

When a dialogue tag comes after a speech, place a comma, exclamation point, or question mark inside the closing quotation marks.

When an attribution tag comes after a direct quote, place a comma, exclamation point, or question mark inside the closing quotation marks.

QUOTATION MARKS

Dialogue is set off by quotation marks.

A quote within a quote is surrounded by single quotation marks.

When a dialogue tag comes after a speech, place a comma, exclamation point, or question mark inside the closing quotation marks.

When a dialogue tag comes before a speech, place a comma after the tag. Put the dialogue's final punctuation mark inside the closing quotation marks.

When an attribution tag comes after a direct quote, place a comma, exclamation point, or question mark inside the closing quotation marks.

Direct quotations are set off by quotation marks.

When an attribution tag comes before a direct quote, place a comma after the tag. Put the dialogue's final punctuation mark inside the closing quotation marks.

When an attribution tag comes in the middle of a direct quotation, follow it with a comma if the remaining quote is an incomplete sentence. Follow it with a period if the remaining quote is a complete sentence.

Use quotation marks for minor or brief works of art and writing or portions of longer works such as short stories, newspaper articles, songs, chapters, and poems.

SEMICOLONS

The independent clauses of a compound sentence must be joined by a comma and a coordinating conjunction, a semicolon, or a semicolon and a coordinating conjunction. They cannot be joined by a comma alone.

If items in a series contain commas within the items, semicolons may separate two or more items in a series.

If semicolons separate items in a series, a colon may set off the series.

SENTENCE PUNCTUATION

A sentence begins with a capital letter and ends with a punctuation mark.
  A statement always ends with a period.
  An exclamation always ends with an exclamation point.
  A command ends with either a period or an exclamation point.
  A question always ends with a question mark.

DOCUMENTATION
(Turabian, with an introduction to other options)

About Turabian

The style described here is the most common one for student papers. It is known as "Turabian," after Kate Turabian, the head secretary for the graduate department at the University of Chicago from 1930 until 1958. Kate Turabian had to approve the format of every doctoral dissertation and master's thesis submitted to the University of Chicago. These papers were supposed to follow the format of the University of Chicago Manual of Style, but the Manual of Style is huge and complicated and many students couldn't figure out exactly how to use it. So Kate Turabian wrote a simplified version of the Manual of Style, intended just for the use of students writing papers. It was called *A Manual for Writers of Research Papers, Theses, and Dissertations*, and her book has sold over eight million copies.

A sentence containing a direct quote should be accompanied by a citation.

A superscript number may lead to a citation at the bottom of the page (a footnote) or the end of the paper (an endnote).

  1) Footnotes and endnotes should follow this format:

    Author name, *Title of Book* (Publisher, year of publication), p. #.

If there are two authors, list them like this:

> Author name and author name, *Title of Book* (Publisher, year of publication), p. #.

If your quote comes from more than one page of the book you're quoting, use "pp." to mean "pages" and put a hyphen between the page numbers.

> Author name, *Title of Book* (Publisher, date of publication), pp. #-#.

If a book is a second (or third, or fourth, etc.) edition, put that information right after the title.

> Author name, *Title of Book*, 2nd ed. (Publisher, date of publication), p. #.

If no author is listed, simply use the title.

> *Title of book* (Publisher, date of publication), p. #.

All of this information can be found on the copyright page of the book.

2) Footnotes should be placed beneath a dividing line at the bottom of the page. If you are using a word-processing program, the font size of the footnotes should be about 2 points smaller than the font size of the main text.

3) Endnotes should be placed at the end of the paper, under a centered heading:

ENDNOTES

[1]Wendy Paul, *101 Gourmet Cookies for Everyone* (Bonneville Books, 2010), p. 18.
[2] Author, *Title of book* (Publisher, year of publication), page number.

For a short paper (three pages or less), the endnotes can be placed on the last page of the paper itself. A paper that is four or more pages in length should have an entirely separate page for endnotes.

4) The second time you cite a book, your footnote or endnote only needs to contain the following information:

[2] Author last name, p. #.

5) If a paragraph contains several quotes from the same source, a single citation at the end of the entire paragraph can cover all quotations.

Every work mentioned in a footnote or endnote must also appear on a final Works Cited page:

WORKS CITED

Paul, Wendy. *101 Gourmet Cookies for Everyone.* Springville, UT: Bonneville Books, 2010.

1) **List sources alphabetically by the author's last name.**

2) **The format should be: Last name, first name. *Title of Book.* City of publication: Publisher, year of publication.**

3) **If the work has no author, list it by the first word of the title (but ignore the articles *a, an*, and *the*).**

4) **If the city of publication is not a major city (New York, Los Angeles, London, Beijing, New Delhi, Tokyo), include the state (for a U.S. publisher) or country (for an international publisher).**

5) **For a short paper (three pages or less), the Works Cited section may be at the bottom of the last page. For a paper of four or more pages, attach a separate Works Cited page.**

Additional Rules for Citing Sources (Turabian)

1) Magazine articles

In a footnote or endnote, use the following style:

[1] Author name, "Name of article." *Name of Magazine*, Date of publication, page number.
[2] Jacqueline Harp, "A Breed for Every Yard: Black Welsh Mountain Sheep Break New Ground." *Sheep!*, September/October 2013, p. 27.

In Works Cited, use the following style:

Author last name, first name. "Name of article." *Name of Magazine* volume number: issue number (Date of publication), total pages article takes up in magazine.

Harp, Jacqueline. "A Breed for Every Yard: Black Welsh Mountain Sheep Break New Ground." *Sheep!* 34:5 (September/October 2013), pp. 26–28.

2) Websites

In a footnote or endnote, use the following style:

[3] Author/editor/sponsoring organization of website, "Name of article," URL (date accessed).
[4] Mallory Daughtery, "Baa Baa Black and White Sheep Treats," http://www.southernliving.com/home-garden/holidays-occasions/spring-table-settings-centerpieces-00400000041389/page8.html (accessed Sept. 12, 2013).

In Works Cited, use the following style:

> Author/editor/sponsoring organization of website. "Name of article."
> URL (date accessed).
> Daughtery, Mallory. "Baa Baa Black and White Sheep Treats." http://
> www.southernliving.com/home-garden/holidays-occasions/spring-
> table-settings-centerpieces-00400000041389/page8.html (accessed Sept.
> 12, 2013).

3) Ebooks with flowing text (no traditional page numbers)

In a footnote or endnote, use the following style:

> [5] Author name, *Name of book* (Publisher, date), Name of ebook format:
> Chapter number, any other information given by ebook platform.
> [6] Paul de Kruif, *Microbe Hunters* (Harvest, 1996), Kindle: Ch. 7, Loc.
> 2134.

In Works Cited, use the following style:

> Author last name, author first name. *Title of book*. City of publication:
> Publisher, date. Name of ebook format.

> de Kruif, Paul. *Microbe Hunters.* Fort Washington, PA: Harvest, 1996.
> Kindle.

In-text citations may be used in scientific or technical writing.

> The chemical reactions that take place within Chocolate Chip Pudding
> Cookies make them "by far the softest chocolate chip cookies" (Paul
> 2010, 18) that can be found.[1]

Alternative Styles for Citation

Turabian (most common for students)

FOOTNOTE/ENDNOTE

[1] Susan Cooper, *Silver on the Tree* (Atheneum, 1977), p. 52.

IN-TEXT CITATION

(Cooper 1977, 52)

WORKS CITED

Cooper, Susan. *Silver on the Tree.* New York: Atheneum, 1977.

Chicago Manual of Style

FOOTNOTE/ENDNOTE

[1] Susan Cooper, *Silver on the Tree* (New York: Atheneum 1977), p. 52.

IN-TEXT CITATION

(Cooper 1977, 52)

WORKS CITED

Cooper, Susan. 1977. *Silver on the Tree*. New York: Atheneum, 1977.

APA (American Psychological Association, the standard for science writing)

FOOTNOTE/ENDNOTE

APA does not recommend the use of footnotes or endnotes.

IN-TEXT CITATION

(Cooper, 1977, p. 52)

WORKS CITED

Cooper, S. (1977). *Silver on the tree*. New York: Atheneum.

MLA (Modern Language Association, more often used in the arts and humanities)

FOOTNOTE/ENDNOTE

MLA does not recommend the use of footnotes or endnotes for citations. They should only be used to direct the reader to additional books or resources that should be consulted.

IN-TEXT CITATION

(Cooper 52)

WORKS CITED

Cooper, Susan. *Silver on the Tree*. New York, NY, United States: Atheneum, 1977. Print.

SAMPLE CONJUGATIONS

Regular Verbs

Indicative

Indicative Simple Tenses

Simple Past

	ACTIVE		PASSIVE	
	Singular	**Plural**	**Singular**	**Plural**
1st person:	I forgot	We forgot	I was forgotten	We were forgotten
2nd person:	You forgot	You forgot	You were forgotten	You were forgotten
3rd person:	He, she, it forgot	They forgot	He, she, it was forgotten	They were forgotten

Simple Present

	ACTIVE		PASSIVE	
	Singular	**Plural**	**Singular**	**Plural**
1st person:	I see	We see	I am seen	We are seen
2nd person:	You see	You see	You are seen	You are seen
3rd person:	He, she, it sees	They see	He, she, it is seen	They are seen

Simple Future

	ACTIVE		PASSIVE	
	Singular	**Plural**	**Singular**	**Plural**
1st person:	I will hear	We will hear	I will be heard	We will be heard
2nd person:	You will hear	You will hear	You will be heard	You will be heard
3rd person:	He, she, it will hear	They will hear	He, she, it will be heard	They will be heard

Indicative Perfect Tenses

Perfect Past

	ACTIVE		PASSIVE	
	Singular	**Plural**	**Singular**	**Plural**
1st person:	I had amused	We had amused	I had been amused	We had been amused
2nd person:	You had amused	You had amused	You had been amused	You had been amused
3rd person:	He, she, it had amused	They had amused	He, she, it had been amused	They had been amused

Perfect Present

	ACTIVE		PASSIVE	
	Singular	**Plural**	**Singular**	**Plural**
1st person:	I have amused	We have amused	I have been amused	We have been amused
2nd person:	You have amused	You have amused	You have been amused	You have been amused
3rd person:	He, she, it has amused	They have amused	He, she, it has been amused	They have been amused

Perfect Future

	ACTIVE		PASSIVE	
	Singular	**Plural**	**Singular**	**Plural**
1st person:	I will have amused	We will have amused	I will have been amused	We will have been amused
2nd person:	You will have amused	You will have amused	You will have been amused	You will have been amused
3rd person:	He, she, it will have amused	They will have amused	He, she, it will have been amused	They will have been amused

Indicative Progressive Tenses

Progressive Past

	ACTIVE		PASSIVE	
	Singular	**Plural**	**Singular**	**Plural**
1st person:	I was asking	We were asking	I was being asked	We were being asked
2nd person:	You were asking	You were asking	You were being asked	You were being asked
3rd person:	He, she, it was asking	They were asking	He, she, it was being asked	They were being asked

Progressive Present

	ACTIVE		PASSIVE	
	Singular	**Plural**	**Singular**	**Plural**
1st person:	I am asking	We are asking	I am being asked	We are being asked
2nd person:	You are asking	You are asking	You are being asked	You are being asked
3rd person:	He, she, it is asking	They are asking	He, she, it is being asked	They are being asked

Progressive Future

	ACTIVE		PASSIVE	
	Singular	**Plural**	**Singular**	**Plural**
1st person:	I will be asking	We will be asking	I will be being asked	We will be being asked
2nd person:	You will be asking	You will be asking	You will be being asked	You will be being asked
3rd person:	He, she, it will be asking	They will be asking	He, she, it will be being asked	They will be being asked

Indicative Progressive Perfect Tenses

Progressive Perfect Past

	ACTIVE		PASSIVE	
	Singular	**Plural**	**Singular**	**Plural**
1st person:	I had been amusing	We had been amusing	I had been being amused	We had been being amused
2nd person:	You had been amusing	You had been amusing	You had been being amused	You had been being amused
3rd person:	He, she, it had been amusing	They had been amusing	He, she, it had been being amused	They had been being amused

Progressive Perfect Present

	ACTIVE		PASSIVE	
	Singular	**Plural**	**Singular**	**Plural**
1st person:	I have been amusing	We have been amusing	I have been being amused	We have been being amused
2nd person:	You have been amusing	You have been amusing	You have been being amused	You have been being amused
3rd person:	He, she, it has been amusing	They have been amusing	He, she, it has been being amused	They have been being amused

Progressive Perfect Future

	ACTIVE		PASSIVE	
	Singular	**Plural**	**Singular**	**Plural**
1st person:	I will have been amusing	We will have been amusing	I will have been being amused	We will have been being amused
2nd person:	You will have been amusing	You will have been amusing	You will have been being amused	You will have been being amused
3rd person:	He, she, it will have been amusing	They will have been amusing	He, she, it will have been being amused	They will have been being amused

Subjunctive

Subjunctive Simple Tenses

Simple Past

	ACTIVE		PASSIVE	
	Singular	**Plural**	**Singular**	**Plural**
1st person:1st	I left	We left	I were left	We were left
etc. (same as indicative simple past)			You were left	You were left
			He, she, it	They were
			were left	left

Simple Present

	ACTIVE		PASSIVE	
	Singular	**Plural**	**Singular**	**Plural**
1st person:	I leave	We leave	I be left	We be left
2nd person:	You leave	You leave	You be left	You be left
3rd person:	He, she, it leave	They leave	He, she it be left	They be left

Simple Future

There is no actual subjunctive form for the future; instead, use the simple past subjunctive state of being verb, plus an infinitive, to express a future unreal action.

	ACTIVE		PASSIVE	
	Singular	**Plural**	**Singular**	**Plural**
1st person:	I were to leave	We were to leave	I were to be left	We were to be left
2nd person:	You were to leave	You were to leave	You were to be left	You were to be left
3rd person:	He, she, it were to leave	They were to leave	He, she, it were to be left	They were to be left

Subjunctive Progressive Tenses

Progressive Past

	ACTIVE		PASSIVE	
	Singular	**Plural**	**Singular**	**Plural**
1st person:	I were scolding	We were scolding	I were being left	We were being left
2nd person:	You were scolding	You were scolding	You were being left	You were being left
3rd person:	He, she, it were scolding	They were scolding	He, she, it were being left	They were being left

Progressive Present

None

Note: Although it is technically possible to form the progressive present subjunctive, English speakers usually use the simple present subjunctive or a gerund/verb combination to express unreal situations in these tenses.

Progressive present subjunctive: *If I be scolding you, stop what you are doing.*
Simple present subjunctive: *If I scold you, stop what you are doing.*
Simple present subjunctive plus gerund: *If I keep on scolding you, stop what you are doing.*

Progressive Future

None

Subjunctive Perfect Tenses

Perfect Past

	ACTIVE		PASSIVE	
	Singular	**Plural**	**Singular**	**Plural**
1st person:	I had left	We had left	I had been left	We had been left

etc. (same as indicative perfect past)

Perfect Present

	ACTIVE		PASSIVE	
	Singular	**Plural**	**Singular**	**Plural**
1st person:	I have left	We have left	I have been left	We have been left

etc. (same as indicative perfect present)

Perfect Future

	ACTIVE	PASSIVE

None

Subjunctive Progressive Perfect Tenses

Progressive Perfect Past

	ACTIVE		PASSIVE	
	Singular	**Plural**	**Singular**	**Plural**
1st	I had been leaving	We had been leaving	I had been being left	We had been being left

etc. (same as indicative progressive perfect past)

Progressive Perfect Present

	ACTIVE		PASSIVE	
	Singular	**Plural**	**Singular**	**Plural**
1st person:	I have been leaving	We have been leaving	I have been being left	We have been being left

etc. (same as indicative progressive perfect present)

Progressive Perfect Future
ACTIVE   *PASSIVE*

None

Modal

Modal Simple Tenses

Simple Past

None

Simple Present

	ACTIVE		PASSIVE	
	Singular	**Plural**	**Singular**	**Plural**
1st person:	I could notice	We should notice	I could be noticed	We should be noticed
2nd person:	You might notice	You must notice	You might be noticed	You must be noticed
3rd person:	He, she, it may notice	They might notice	He, she, it may be noticed	They might be noticed

Simple Future

None

Modal Perfect Tenses

Perfect Past

None

Perfect Present

	ACTIVE		PASSIVE	
	Singular	**Plural**	**Singular**	**Plural**
1st person:	I could have noticed	We should have noticed	I could have been noticed	We should have been noticed
2nd person:	You might have noticed	You must have noticed	You might have been noticed	You must have been noticed
3rd person:	He, she, it may have noticed	They might have noticed	He, she, it may have been noticed	They might have been noticed

Perfect Future

None

Modal Progressive Tenses

Progressive Past

None

Progressive Present

	ACTIVE		PASSIVE	
	Singular	**Plural**	**Singular**	**Plural**
1st person:	I could be taking	We should be taking	I could be being taken	We should be being taken
2nd person:	You might be taking	You must be taking	You might be being taken	You must be being taken
3rd person:	He, she, it may be taking	They might be taking	He, she, it may be being taken	They might be being taken

Progressive Future

None

Modal Progressive Perfect Tenses

Progressive Perfect Past

None

Progressive Perfect Present

	ACTIVE		PASSIVE	
	Singular	**Plural**	**Singular**	**Plural**
1st person:	I could have been washing	We should have been washing	I could have been being washed	We should have been being washed
2nd person:	You might have been washing	You must have been washing	You might have been being washed	You must have been being washed
3rd person:	He, she, it may have been washing	They might have been washing	He, she, it may have been being washed	They might have been being washed

Progressive Perfect Future

None

Imperatives

ACTIVE	PASSIVE
Finish!	Be finished! [See "hortative"]

Hortatives

	ACTIVE		PASSIVE	
	Singular	**Plural**	**Singular**	**Plural**
1st person:	——	Let us exhort	——	Let us be exhorted
2nd person:	May you exhort	May you exhort	May you be exhorted	May you be exhorted
3rd person:	Let him exhort	May they exhort	Let her be exhorted	May they be exhorted

Infinitives

Simple Infinitives

Simple Past

None

Simple Present

ACTIVE	*PASSIVE*
to hear	to be heard

Simple Future

None

Perfect Infinitives

Perfect Past

None

Perfect Present

ACTIVE	*PASSIVE*
to have heard	to have been heard

Perfect Future

None

Progressive Infinitives

Progressive Past

None

Progressive Present

ACTIVE	*PASSIVE*
to be hearing	to be being heard

Progressive Future

None

Progressive Perfect Infinitives

Progressive Perfect Past

None

Progressive Perfect Present

ACTIVE	*PASSIVE*
to have been hearing	to have been being heard

Progressive Perfect Future

None

State of Being Verbs

Simple Tenses

Simple Past

	Indicative		*Subjunctive*	
	Singular	**Plural**	**Singular**	**Plural**
1st person:	I was	We were	I were	We were
2nd person:	You were	You were	You were	You were
3rd person:	He, she, it was	They were	He, she, it were	They were

Simple Present

	Indicative		*Subjunctive*	
	Singular	**Plural**	**Singular**	**Plural**
1st person:	I am	We are	I be	We be
2nd person:	You are	You are	You be	You be
3rd person:	He, she, it is	They are	He, she, it be	They be

Simple Future

	Indicative		*Subjunctive*
	Singular	**Plural**	
1st person:	I will be	We will be	*same as indicative*
2nd person:	You will be	You will be	
3rd person:	He, she, it will be	They will be	

Perfect Tenses

Perfect Past

	Indicative		*Subjunctive*
	Singular	**Plural**	
1st person:	I had been	We had been	*same as indicative*
2nd person:	You had been	You had been	
3rd person:	He, she, it had been	They had been	

Perfect Present

	Indicative		*Subjunctive*
	Singular	**Plural**	
1st person:	I have been	We have been	*same as indicative*
2nd person:	You have been	You have been	
3rd person:	He, she, it has been	They have been	

Perfect Future

	Indicative		*Subjunctive*
	Singular	**Plural**	
1st person:	I will have been	We will have been	*same as indicative*
2nd person:	You will have been	You will have been	
3rd person:	He, she, it will have been	They will have been	

Progressive Tenses

Progressive Past

	Indicative		*Subjunctive*
	Singular	**Plural**	
1st person:	I was being	We were being	*same as indicative*
2nd person:	You were being	You were being	
3rd person:	He, she, it was being	They were being	

Progressive Present

	Indicative		*Subjunctive*
1st person:	I am being	We are being	*same as indicative*
2nd person:	You are being	You are being	
3rd person:	He, she, it is being	They are being	

Progressive Future

	Indicative		*Subjunctive*
1st person:	I will be being	We will be being	*same as indicative*
2nd person:	You will be being	You will be being	
3rd person:	He, she, it will be being	They will be being	

Progressive Perfect Tenses

Perfect Past

	Indicative		*Subjunctive*
1st person:	I had been being	We had been being	*same as indicative*
2nd person:	You had been being	You had been being	
3rd person:	He, she, it had been being	They had been being	

Perfect Present

	Indicative		*Subjunctive*
1st person:	I have been being	We have been being	*same as indicative*
2nd person:	You have been being	You have been being	
3rd person:	He, she, it has been being	They have been being	

Perfect Future

	Indicative		*Subjunctive*
1st person:	I will have been being	We will have been being	*same as indicative*
2nd person:	You will have been being	You will have been being	
3rd person:	He, she, it will have been being	They will have been being	

INDEX